THE CALIFORNIA CONDITION
A Pregnant Architecture

Organized by the La Jolla Museum of Contemporary Art
November 13, 1982 - January 2, 1983

Supported by Grants from the National Endowment for the Arts, a Federal Agency, the
Graham Foundation for Advanced Studies in the Fine Arts and assistance from Formica Corporation.

CONTENTS

To John Dymock Entenza whose perceptions about and allegiance to California architects in the 1940's, 1950's and 1960's helped communicate the pluralistic principles so commonly taken for granted in the west. His well documented support of American and particularly California architects, initially through his mentorship of *Arts & Architecture* and later as Director of the Graham Foundation for Advanced Studies in the Fine Arts, made possible a climate in which an exhibition and catalogue such as this could be possible.

DIRECTOR'S FOREWARD

Observers of architecture in this country and in Europe agree that some highly original and important work is being created by architects in California. The purpose of this exhibition is to apprise the public of recent developments in architecture in California through a balanced and comprehensive exhibition. It was my feeling that an unbiased perspective was needed, so I invited Chicago-based architect Stanley Tigerman and New York-based architecture writer Susan Grant Lewin (now Creative Director of Formica Corporation, she was formerly Architecture Editor of *House Beautiful*). The curators have selected the architects not only because of the intrinsic merit of their works, but also because of the influence of and interest in their work beyond this region. I would like to thank them for curating the exhibition and for their perceptive catalogue essays.

This exhibition contains the work of thirteen talented architects and architectural teams from San Diego, Los Angeles and San Francisco. The work, presented in the form of drawings and models, communicates the ideas and philosophies of these provocative architects. It is my conviction that these architects are also artists and that their works properly belong in a museum context. I thank them for wholeheartedly responding to our invitation to participate in this exhibition.

We appreciate the support of the National Endowment for the Arts, the Graham Foundation for Advanced Studies in the Fine Arts and Formica Corporation.

I would like to take this opportunity to express special thanks to Curator Lynda Forsha for coordinating this exhibition, to former Chief Curator Robert McDonald for editing the catalogue texts, and to Curatorial Assistant Connie O'Neal for her exceptional support in all phases of this project.

Rarely does any discipline have the energy injected into its lifeline that occurred when John Entenza was active in this great profession. I am personally indebted to him and pleased that we can dedicate this exhibition to this great man.

SEBASTIAN J. ADLER
Director

GUEST CURATORS' ACKNOWLEDGMENTS

We wish to thank the La Jolla Museum of Contemporary Art for recognizing the value of the exhibition in the first place and in particular Sebastian Adler, who prodded it into realization. The many architects included unselfishly spent their time (and in some cases their money) in order to respond adequately to our several requests for reviewing their work. We would also like to thank John Chase for his carefully considered comments and Irene Hoehl for her assistance. The staff of the Museum was most cooperative, particularly Curator Lynda Forsha, who coordinated this entire venture, and former Chief Curator Robert McDonald and Marina LaPalma, who edited the texts. Without the early financial support of the Graham Foundation for Advanced Studies in the Fine Arts, and in particular Carter H. Manny, Jr., the exhibition would not have been possible. In addition, we wish to thank the National Endowment for the Arts for its grant.

STANLEY TIGERMAN   SUSAN GRANT LEWIN

CURATOR'S ACKNOWLEDGMENTS

An exhibition of this complexity is only realized through the support and cooperation of many people. Director Sebastian J. Adler initiated this exhibition and delegated to me the responsibilities for coordinating it and producing the catalogue. I am especially grateful to Guest Curators Stanley Tigerman and Susan Grant Lewin, whom Mr. Adler asked to select the architects and write the catalogue essays.

We would like to express our gratitude to the architects for their enthusiasm and spirit and for their diligence in producing the projects for the exhibition and this catalogue. The architects are also the lenders to the exhibition, and we are grateful for their cooperation.

I would like to take this opportunity to thank the people who worked most closely with me on this exhibition: former Chief Curator Robert McDonald for editing the texts and supporting me in many aspects of this exhibition; Curatorial Assistant Connie O'Neal, for her indispensable assistance in every stage of the exhibition coordination and catalogue production; and Registrar Bolton Colburn for handling with great skill his part in organizing this exhibition and the catalogue checklist.

Others whose help I wish to acknowledge are Marina LaPalma for her assistance in editing the texts and Interns Laura Rohrer and Leah Goldman for their many hours of attention to detail.

I wish to express my thanks to Mary Farris for the design of the catalogue and to Photographer John Durant for many of the images in it. The contributions of both are exemplary in quality.

Other members of the Museum staff I would especially like to thank, are Janet Ciaffone, Administrative Assistant; Racthel Lindgren, Financial Officer; Prudence Hutshing, Information Officer; Michael Golino, Building Manager; Robert Schueler, Auditorium Manager; Robin Bright, Preparator; Russell Hilbert, Woodshop Manager; Jill Riveroll, Receptionist; and Shannon Spiess, Membership Coordinator.

LYNDA FORSHA
Curator

THE CALIFORNIA CONDITION

More than anything else, *The California Condition* is a sensuous exaggeration of the American condition. Perhaps the generally held belief about California's ideal weather lulls us into a state of forgetfulness about the "imminence-of-the-earthquake" and other circumstances of impermanence, Hollywood, for example. Nevertheless, *The FABULOUS California Condition* is never very far from our minds.

Thus, when the Director of the La Jolla Museum of Contemporary Art asked me to curate an exhibition of the work of California architects, I was delighted. It fascinated me, a "foreigner," to mull over certain compelling cultural factors of a region where sirens sing idyllic myths for the entire country. Somewhat suspicious at having been selected to organize the exhibit, I accepted the task with the thought that my geographical (if not emotional) distance might mitigate some of the usual difficulties connected with such a show.

One traditional method for analyzing the work of artists and architects is the convention of Hegelian cultural overlay.[1] Hegel's attitude was that art can only be understood by absorbing the culture for which it was made, and, since civilization is always in flux, art (which Plato observed is but a shadow of the truth) is also perpetually in flux. Thus, implicit in Hegel's argument is the conclusion that one is never presented with a finished result but always confronts a work of art as a point in an ongoing, dialectical cultural process.

Now, it seems to me that California represents a state of mind that is, to borrow a phrase from Kierkegaard, "in the process of becoming." There was simply no place farther west to go when Horace Greeley said, "Go west, young man"; and since one can never dispose of the phenomena of memory, the California condition reflects, often inadvertently, the pluralistic (or just plain perversely) disparate strains of changing American interests. Clearly, looking backwards has a romantic significance, and, if nothing else, California is romantic. Now romanticism enlarged through exaggeration is often referred to as "kitsch," which is another accusation often leveled at California and Californians.

The motion of turning the head backward while the body is moving forward often implies semantic reverie rather than syntactic leadership. California is guilty of this, too, since intrinsic artistic development in that state is, more often than not, absorbed and regurgitated in extrinsically symbolic rather than syntactically integral ways. The urge to expand upon

---

1.   Renowned art historian Ernst Gombrich states: "It is my belief that Hegel is the father of the history of art, or at any rate of the history of art as I have always understood it." *In* "Hegel and Art History," *Architectural Design*, vol. 51, no. 6/7 (1981), issue entitled *On the Methodology of Architectural History*, pp. 3-9.

the semantic rather than the syntactic comes easily to California, since it is the grist of the place — after all, the making and the communicating of semantic symbols is the very life blood of HOLLYWOOD. Which brings me back to my thoughts about California and exaggeration.

I would further contend that, since the monotonously ideal weather not only permits the construction of things to be left out in the rain but correspondingly simplifies related conceptual activities, much of the customary, if self-assumed, complexity assigned to architecture by many architects is, in California terms, eschewed in favor of even greater concentration on the purely semantic. But, let's face it, things, movements and otherwise, do not just move westward — they may, through synthesis, reverse their field and be re-absorbed into the mainstream of American culture that banished them in the first place. Thus, the California kitchen, the family room, the carport and many more of those familiar forms of a culture struggling to return to a state of nature have both planted the seeds and then reaped the fruits of an architecture enriched by California sunshine.

But that's just it — California is, above all, a place where the recognition of the individual in his or her most idiosyncratically exaggerated form is celebrated. If, as Hegel believed, art can best be understood by the culture for which it is made and which it reflects, then as one girds one's typewriter for an analytical attack on architects of various persuasions throughout the state (both of mind and of place), the Hegelian method seems particularly appropriate. Which brings us to the subject at hand: those strange creatures — the bathing beauties of American architecture — California architects, individually and collectively.

The selection procedure for this exhibition was not based on the desire to reward, but rather on representativeness. It is my belief that one could replace the architects selected with an equal number of exhibitors two or three times over and still reasonably display the several strains of stylistic and technical prodigiousness common to this state.

It is not my purpose, therefore, to celebrate particularly those architects selected for exhibition by dwelling only on their individual proficiencies (or delinquencies). Indeed, their selection was intended to show the historical connections implicit in each of several directions defined by their work. The result is that this essay will attempt to deal with these exhibitors not simply by dissecting their work but by relating it both to their peers and their predecessors in order to examine what unique and strange forces are at work in the West.

The California Condition fascinates me because it represents a position completely opposite to the normative thought central to the architects of my own city hard by this inland sea. By revealing both my background and my bias, I hope to make clear where I am coming from, since I do not have Socratic distance from a subject such as this. Neither, however, is this a polemic, since I have nothing to prove nor any axes to grind. But I do have rather definite opinions about the state of the art of California architecture which I hope to make clear.

There are four large-scale classifications by which one might reasonably cluster architects and architectural production for the purpose of aesthetic speculation. Each general category, in turn, is then divided into sub-groups — two in the first, three in the second, three in the third, and two in the fourth — thus, they are suitably and symmetrically arranged. Perhaps this is the Fates at work, since my reasoning is that California is simply not as open-ended a condition as one might believe, but rather it is more pre-conceived than purely conceptual in its composition.

The first general organizing device I have established has somewhat earlier antecedents than subsequent sections; as such, it is more deeply rooted in the material, stylistic and ethnic origins of the state. Predominantly historical in origin, this device is not without illusory connotations. I have entitled this category *Historic Regionalism* and I have arranged two sub-sections within this larger definition — the first addresses historical illusion as well as both Mission Style and Spanish Colonial architecture, and the second attempts to contend with what has largely come to be known as Bay Area architecture (though, certainly not all of its proponents practice their craft in the San Francisco region). Antecedent figures within the first sub-section include Bernard Maybeck and Irving Gill, with current practitioners Charles Moore (Moore Ruble Yudell), Langdon and Wilson and Thomas Gordon Smith. The second sub-section owes a major debt to Frank Lloyd Wright, with inevitable curtsies to the Brothers Greene, William Wilson Wurster and John Lautner. Contemporary carriers of this wood-burning flame include William Turnbull, Jr., Donlyn Lyndon and from far south in the state, Martinez/Wong.

Since the second organizing classification has more recent origins than the first, representing California architects' responses to, and interpretations of, schismatic modernist attitudes, and since many of those attitudes were steeped in presumably logical and egalitarian replacements of earlier princely modes, I have labeled this section *Pragmatic Modernism*. It consists of three sub-sections, the first of which addresses canonical modernist tendencies as first articulated by Le Corbusier, with regional interpreters such as Rudolph Schindler, Richard Neutra, J.R. Davidson and Harwell Hamilton Harris. More recent advocates of this position include Frank Tomsik, Daniel Dworsky and Marquis and Stoller, with contemporary figures such as Roland Coate (the architect, not the artist), Lomax/Rock and Daniel Solomon/Barbara Stauffacher-Solomon rounding out this sub-section. The second sub-section attempts to clarify the case of mindless Mies modernism bereft of the rigor of Mies van der Rohe's presence. As such, it quite naturally refers back to that great twentieth-century master himself as the overriding, larger-than-life, antecedent figure in this category. Other more practical-minded proponents of this epochal approach to architecture were Konrad Wachsmann, Craig Ellwood, Charles Eames and Raphael Soriano. Many of John Entenza's Case Study House Program authors such as Pierre Koenig, A. Quincy Jones and Ed Killingsworth, with more recent architects of this persuasion such as James Pulliam, Bernard Zimmerman, A.C. Martin, Gene Summers (a recent student emigre from Miesland Chicago), Helmut Schulitz and Peter de Bretteville, constitute this obviously popular (and equally obviously Southern California based) bastion. In this category certain architectural schools have institutionalized this modernist mode: both the University of Southern California and the Southern California Institute of Architecture (SCIARC) are predominant among those having tunnel vision in this particular arena. The third and final sub-section here represents "artful pragmatic capitalism" in the form of late modernist (but Eric Mendelsohn inspired) depression-moderne, extruded (and potentially alienating), reflective-glass architecture. While Schindler, Neutra, Kem Weber and J.R. Davidson are plausible progenitors here, this mode is relatively contemporary even in its origins. Cesar Pelli, Tony Lumsden and Paul Kennon were early pursuers of this Didionesque architecture, with later designers Marc Goldstein, Welton Becket, the Lomax/Rock firm and even the recent addition of Jon Thogmartin rounding out this list.

The third overall classification owes much both to the techniques and the sociology of pragmatic building and housing. While this category may be a reasonable extension of much preceding corporate work, this section also begins to address the joint issues of marketing and communication and includes larger issues of formal manipulation and even attempts to embrace the recent phenomenon, "Attitude." I have anointed it with the title: *Manipulated Materialism*. The first of its three sub-sections embraces pragmatic housing with father figures such as Marquis/Stoller, Ray Kappe and Fisher/Friedman as well as MLTW/Turnbull Associates. As this sub-section evolves in a more communicative direction, such architects as John Jerde (with appropriate marketing twists sometimes supplied by Richard Saul Wurman) make their debut; and, as high-style Southern California responses to the singles and the beach front crowd, both Rob Quigley and Martinez/Wong appear. The second sub-section dwells a bit more on the agonizingly contrived forms cajoled into existence by those architects obviously influenced by HOLLYWOOD: the formal manipulators, deco-tech tricksters and a general grab bag of post-modernists. An early advocate of such stylish trends was Tim Vreeland, quickly followed by Eugene Kupper, Eric Owen Moss, Michael Franklin Ross, Batter/Kay and Martinez/Wong. And finally in the third sub-section, the more recent trends toward Funk, Punk, New Wave and Attitude are here represented by Ace Architects, Thomas Grondona and Ted Smith.

Since the final large-scale category represents the opposite side of the coin from the prior group (i.e., dematerialism vs. materialism), and since it is by far, for me, the most avant-garde, I have chosen to label it the *Dematerialized (Disappearing?) Cutting Edge.* The first of two sub-sections owes much of its allegiance both to European-originated, neo-rationalist and post-functionalist tendencies as they have influenced and then been interpreted by the architects of the West Coast. Indeed, many of the proponents of this work are actually foreign born. Such architects as Lars Lerup, Stanley Saidewitz, Andrew Batey and Mark Mack together with Morphosis (Michael Rotondi, Thom Mayne) best represent these internationally contemporaneous concerns. The last sub-section in this final category argues the case of conceptual art and has the dual antecedents of Hollywood-as-conceptual-abstraction and Southern California artists such as Sam Francis, Ed Ruscha, Ron Davis, etc. The major architectural father-figure here is, of course, Frank O. Gehry, with Hodgetts/Mangurian, Coy Howard, Fred Fisher, Frank Israel, and Roland Coate (the artist, not the architect) as disciples and/or descendants.

Within these four large classifications it is my intention to illuminate *The California Condition* rather than to speculate, except by implication, as to which of several possible futures it might have.

HISTORIC REGIONALISM

While California's century-long flirtation with the Renaissance and its re-interpretation within the wood technology common to the region have been endlessly celebrated, Bernard Maybeck's work perhaps comes closest to merging these interests in an architectural amalgam sufficiently unique to defy simplistic classification. The Palace of Fine Arts, San Francisco (1915), perhaps best exemplifies Maybeck's bent for Renaissance interpretation, but his Christian Science Church (1910)[2] and the Kennedy House, (1923) [3] both in Berkeley, better reflect his unique

2. Esther Mc Coy, *Five California Architects* (Praeger Publishers, Inc., New York, N.Y. 1975), p. 27.

3. *Ibid.,* p. 51.

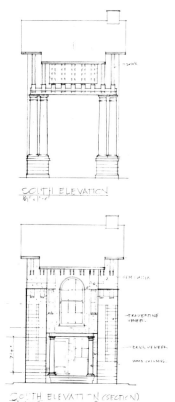

SOUTH ELEVATION

SOUTH ELEVATION (SECTION)

FIG. 1

capability for melding the American vernacular residential tradition with his life-long fascination with antiquity. Of some interest here is the relationship of the facade of the proposed house in Richmond Hills (1982) by Thomas Gordon Smith (Fig. 1) to certain aspects of Maybeck's Christian Science Church and the Kennedy House. In all three cases the symmetry of the public facade overrides other considerations. Nonetheless, each of these three facades is eroded (or embellished, depending upon your point of view) by plan configurations and, therefore, aspects of movement which complicate yet ultimately enrich one's initial reaction to each. If Maybeck's historicizing, chronologically speaking, is at the front door of the Renaissance, then T.G. Smith's fascinations lie at its back door, for while much of Maybeck's formal borrowing comes from Gothic and Romanesque proto-Renaissance forms, a great deal of Smith's eclecticism stems from his interest in the Baroque, particularly the architecture of Carlo Fontana, Francesco Borromini and Carlo Maderno. And yet there is a curious overlap between the hulking, bear-like romanticism of Maybeck and the zealous affinity Smith has for Baroque formal manipulation. I would suggest it is the curious combination of California's geographic distance from European forcefulness, along with a perverse desire to reinterpret the Aryan side of its cultural origins, that is at the heart of this alien amalgam. California is, in a word, schizophrenic.

If architectural schizophrenia is an old friend both to Maybeck and T.G. Smith, it is even more intimately related to Irving Gill and Langdon and Wilson. If Gill's technologically motivated method of constructing the tilt slab La Jolla Women's Club (1913)[4] is at the service of a classically derivative building, then Langdon and Wilson's J. Paul Getty Museum at Malibu (1970-75),[5] less technologically and constructionally based, is at once more literally reminiscent (in this case, of Herculaneum). Both, however, bring to *The California Condition* attitudes about another time and another civilization's architecture.

Perhaps no single architect today in California or anywhere else is able to merge feelings about historic illusionism, and with it a sense of high theatre, and our consumer-oriented society better than Charles Moore. Together with John Ruble and Buzz Yudell in the design of the Rodes House in Brentwood (1976-79)[6] they couple Baroque plan forms with

4.   *Ibid.*, pp. 78-82.

5.   Charles Jencks, *The Language of Post-Modern Architecture* (Rizzoli International, New York, N.Y., 1977), p. 82.

6.   Charles Jencks, *Post Modern Classicism* (Garden House Press, Academy Editions, London, 1980), pp. 28-29.

FIG. 2

FIG. 3

symmetry and use exaggerated fenestration to convey scale shifts with theatrical panache, thus establishing great presence in this otherwise modest house. (Fig. 2) The fact is that Moore Ruble Yudell is almost without peer in contemporarily presenting both Mission Style and Spanish Colonial architecture.

It is impossible within the context of historic regionalism to overlook Frank Lloyd Wright's influence on Bay Area architecture and, for that matter, the extended use of wood as a rational approach to residential problem-solving. A contemporary self-anointed descendant of Wright is John Lautner, but the use of wood, both structurally and decoratively embellished, can also be attributed far earlier to Charles Sumner Greene and Henry Mather Greene. Their formal connection to Wright is evidenced by, among many others, the L.A. Robinson House in Pasadena (1906),[7] although the David B. Gamble house, also in Pasadena (1908),[8] is more idiosyncratically representative of their own style. More contemporary is the 1940's and 1950's work of William Wilson Wurster, who, with Theodore Bernardi, established a post-World War II California contemporaneity equalled only by the third career of George Howe on the East Coast[9] and by the second career of George Fred Keck in the Middle West.[10] While the bulk of Wurster's oeuvre had a decidedly indigenous Bay Area cast to it, on occasion it fell prey to the mannerisms of the times — witness his Case Study House,[11] originally planned in 1945, which simply used wood as a structural material without invoking the laid-back Wrightian vernacular characteristic of the bulk of his career.

Of all the contemporary Californians, none epitomizes the American vernacular residential tradition better than William Turnbull, Jr. Beginning with his renowned Zimmerman House (1974-76),[12] familiarly known as the Lattice House, his work has exemplified a side of the original MLTW collaboration that none of his former partners have as doggedly dwelt upon, namely, the American residential vernacular wood tradition. Turnbull's recent Fisher Winery project, Sonoma County (1979-80) (Fig. 3),

7.   McCoy, *op. cit.*, p. 111.

8.   *Ibid.*, pp. 112-123.

9.   Robert A.M. Stern, *George Howe, Toward a Modern American Architecture* (Yale University Press, New Haven and London, 1975), fig. 109-129.

10.   Narcisco G. Menocal, *Keck & Keck Architects* (Elvehjem Museum of Art, University of Wisconsin at Madison, 1980), pp. 46-68.

11.   Esther McCoy, *Case Study Houses, 1945-1962*, second edition (Hennesey and Ingalls, Los Angeles, Ca., 1977), pp. 50-53.

12.   La Biennale di Venezia, *The Presence of the Past* (Electa, Milan, Italy, 1980), p. 316.

FIG. 4

FIG. 5

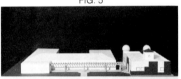
FIG. 6

extends the genre he began with the Zimmerman House, and modifies that emerging tradition in the Davidow House in Kauai, Hawaii, replacing lattice with an abundance of expressed, and apparently structural, wooden joints. (Fig. 4)

Some of the vernacular qualities evident in Turnbull's recent work can predictably be observed in at least one of his former collaborator's housing projects as well. Donlyn Lyndon's 1982 Phoenix Place Project (Fig. 5) in Fair Oaks reveals the vernacular tradition to be alive and well, though in Lyndon's case, and others of this persuasion as well, little else is offered for analysis.

More interesting is at least a portion of the recent work of the San Diego firm of Martinez/Wong Associates. The Joslyn Center Annex at Escondido (1982) (Fig. 6) shows the wood vernacular tradition combined with modernized Mission Style architecture in a way that suggests merging stylistic directions.

PRAGMATIC MODERNISM

The combination of the influences of Frank Lloyd Wright and Le Corbusier has had no more successful amalgam, to my way of thinking, than in California. The reasons for this are twofold: Rudolph Schindler and Richard Neutra. Both were initially trained in Vienna, and both were for a time employed by Wright. They were, however, not the only middle-European immigrants to settle in California. Another early arrival, Kem Weber, came to California in early 1914 to supervise work on the German Pavilion at the Pan-Pacific Exposition. He stayed on after the war broke out and reached Los Angeles in 1921. Another underrated architect from abroad was J.R. Davidson. These talented men established a basis for modernism that would not otherwise have been possible — particularly at the time that their influence began to be felt. Of all of these immigrants, it was Schindler, in my judgment, who had the most pervasive Corbusian influence on the next generation of similarly motivated architects. Not only in his famous Lovell Beach House in Newport Beach (1925-26),[13] but in his houses both for D. Grokowsky in South Pasadena (1928)[14] and W.E. Oliver in Los Angeles (1933),[15] as well as the much later Rose L. Harris House in Los

---

13.   David Gebhard, *Schindler*, A Studio Book (The Viking Press, New York, 1971), pp. 80-89.

14.   *Ibid.*, p. 107.

15.   *Ibid.*, p. 127.

Angeles (1942),[16] his use of cubic solids combines De Stijlian invention with Corbusian overtones and even now conveys that side of canonical modernism separated from extravagant (and often self-indulgent) transparency. Many California architects, compelled by the fashionable pull of modernist concepts, were influenced far more by Schindler than by Neutra as canonical modernism found a home in California. Contemporary with Schindler, but without his stylish influence, was Harwell Hamilton Harris, who in his house for John Entenza in Santa Monica Canyon (1937)[17] was clearly more concerned with the manipulation of opaque surfaces than with either structural expression or transparency. Another example of a project influenced by Schindler was the house by Richard Lind in Los Angeles (1939),[18] which again manipulated solids rather than voids. This influence did not diminish with the coming of World War II, rather it accelerated in the 1950's and the 1960's and, in a somewhat reduced way, is still at work today in California.

One of the most interesting cases in the 1960's of an architect temporarily influenced by the manipulation of cubic solids is Frank O. Gehry, who in his studio for Louis Danziger in Hollywood (1968)[19] extends the genre a bit before he radically shifts direction toward another emerging California strain. (See the section entitled *The Dematerialized Cutting Edge.*)

Also representative of architects swayed by these particular modernist concerns is Daniel Dworsky, who throughout the late 1950's and early 1960's published many projects in *Arts and Architecture* expressing these motivations. Marquis/Stoller also falls into this category, though recognition predominantly came to them for their work in pragmatic housing as an extension of problem-solving, post-"team-ten" concerns. Literal Corbusian cubist opacity, however, reached its zenith with the Alexander House, Montecito (1975), by Roland Coate,[20] who with this project took the genre a final step beyond regional implications. After this, Coate changed not only direction but disciplines as he moved from architecture to painting.[21]

The recent work of Lomax/Rock and Daniel Solomon/Barbara

16.   *Ibid.*, p. 157.

17.   David Gebhard and Harriette von Breton, *L.A. in the 30's* (Peregrine Smith, Lake City, Utah, 1975), p. 146.

18.   *Ibid.*, p. 147 (ill. 155).

19.   Reyner Banham, *Los Angeles, The Architecture of Four Ecologies* (Harper and Row Publishers, New York, Evanston, London), pp. 197-199.

20.   *Progressive Architecture*, vol. LVII, no. 8, (August, 1976), cover and pp. 58-61.

21.   Another architect who shifted from architecture to art, as we shall see, is Craig Ellwood.

FIG. 7

Stauffacher-Solomon shows that modernism is not just a residual force in California. The Lomax Residence and the brilliantly symmetrical town-house infill project in San Francisco by Solomon/Stauffacher-Solomon (Fig. 7) show that more than just the frame or layered transparency have distinct possibilities for exploration in this category. Recent projects by Frank Tomsik (after the departure of his former partner Gerald McCue, who became Dean of the Graduate School of Design at Harvard University) reinforce this movement, and after some years Dworsky himself has refined his efforts in this direction.[22]

As Reyner Banham said about the neo-Miesian craze that swept California in the 1940's and 1950's, it was, "The Style that Nearly . . . ."[23] California architects were sufficiently distanced, I would contend, from the source of the flame that they were able to image the semantic symbolism connected with Mies van der Rohe and his work while avoiding the syntactic rigor demanded by proximity to the Master. In hindsight, one could even be persuaded to connect lightweight steel construction more with Neutra than with Mies; indeed, Neutra's influence in this area is not to be ignored. Even Schindler (and before him Gill) was fascinated by the technological implications of prefabrication. But hindsight must by definition be inclusive, and one simply cannot avoid either the fact or the presence of such Miesian determinist architects as Craig Ellwood, Paffard Clay and Gene Summers, the last two of whom are more recent (and thus more consciously parochial) immigrants.

Actually, the craze for lightweight steel prefabricated construction resulting from the Case Study Program initiated by John Entenza as editor of *Arts and Architecture* came into its own in part through the efforts of Charles Eames in the design both of his own house and the adjacent one for John Entenza in Pacific Palisades (1949).[24] Even earlier, however, were the industrialized building experiments conducted during World War II by Konrad Wachsmann.[25] Yet all of these efforts somehow lacked the rigorous aesthetic tenacity of Mies van der Rohe himself, who, it is common knowledge, would spend hours studying a single detail or concentrating on the proportion of bays modulated by steel H-section

22.   *Architecture and Culture, Los Angeles 2*, Architectural Design 52, Academy Editions, 1982, see photograph p. 103.

23.   Banham, *op. cit.*, p. 223.

24.   McCoy, *Case Study Houses*, pp. 54-61.

25.   Konrad Wachsmann, *The Turning Point of Building, Structure and Design* (Reinhold, New York, 1961).

mullions. Furthermore, since Mies brought to the United States two decades of studies connected with concepts ultimately translatable into industrialized terms, he was never at a loss for ways to absorb the idiosyncratic or unusual into his overriding architectural vocabulary. Not so in California, where the idiosyncratic becomes, through repetition, normative thought, where architecture is more semantically responsive than syntactically original. Ultimately, Mies was less pragmatic than Konrad Wachsmann, for example, who is more akin to the likes of Buckminster Fuller; that is, the technological imperative in Washcmann's hands always seemed to outweigh what Mies called "the spirit of the age."

Now, it might be argued that the "spirit of the age" in California terms is practicality, in which case architects such as Ellwood, Eames, Koenig and Soriano might fit somewhat better into a catalogue of those connected with steel construction. The 1960's work of Pulliam, Zimmerman and Matthews[26] (now Pulliam/Matthews and Associates, Architects) is more understandable when one sees the direction Bernard Zimmerman has followed (pragmatic housing) combined with recent projects of Pulliam/Matthews.[27]

Similarly, early Case Study projects by A. Quincy Jones and Ed Killingsworth suffered radical modification through the years as it became clear that the Mies imperative in California hands was seen stylistically rather than as anything approaching a *Zeitgeist*. It is fair, however, to point out that, Killingsworth, at least, was equally influenced by Paul Rudolph (himself an admitted, though modified, descendant of Mies). Killingsworth, Brady and Smith's Triad Development in La Jolla[28] is clearly influenced by some of the early Rudolph residential work in Sarasota, Florida.

It was as if the Mies method (bereft of syntactic rigor) had finally found a place to squat. Early practitioners of the craft were Raphael Soriano and Pierre Koenig, both of whom used this technique more as a replacement for wood than as a means to develop a modern architectural language, as Mies himself did. Being lightweight, both wood and steel are equally logical choices for use in seismic zones, though steel is more appropriate as a flexure material. Soriano was among the first in the Case Study Program to

26.   Esther McCoy, "19, Young Architects in the United States," *Zodiac 13 International Magazine of Contemporary Architecture* Italy (1963), pp. 191-193.

27.   *Architecture and Culture, Los Angeles 2,* Architectural Design 52, Academy Editions, 1982, see photograph p. 102.

28.   Killingsworth, Brady and Smith, "Development, La Jolla," in McCoy, *Case Study Houses,* pp. 166-188.

leap from wood to steel.[29] There is something extraordinary about California that vitiates even the most solidly sycophantic. The joint cases of Paffard Clay and Gene Summers are interesting in that both, before coming to California, were dyed-in-the-wool Miesians, yet both, shortly after arriving at the Pacific's edge, dramatically modified their architectural behaviors. Clay's work radically changed direction toward a Corbusian stance. Both his San Francisco Art Institute and San Francisco State Student Union projects reflect these tendencies. In his Orange County Industrial Center project Summers becomes more pragmatic in his use of prefabricated building panels than in the refined proportions of the extruded and rolled steel and aluminum elements that constituted the palette he used in Chicago for the office of Mies van der Rohe and later while he was design partner at C.F. Murphy Associates. In a way, both these immigrants harken back to my earlier points about Schindler's De Stijlian and Corbusian manipulation of solids (in the case of Clay), and about Gill, Schindler and Neutra's fascination with the tilt-up panel exercise (in the case of Summers).

More recently, Craig Ellwood,[30] before his career shift, completed his brilliant Art Center College of Design in Pasadena;[31] Helmut Schulitz finished his own house;[32] and Peter de Bretteville continues to work in the idiom of lightweight steel construction. All are rather high-tech and all rather datedly refer to Eames' seminal house rather than to the more rigorous Miesian demands common to those still "in court."

It is a very short commercial step from these vaguely connected modernist tendencies to corporate capitalism. Less because of Schindler and Neutra and more because of Kem Weber and J.R. Davidson, whose designs generally inhabited the world of commerce, and most significantly because of the commercial projects of Eric Mendelsohn in pre-World War II Berlin (Mendelsohn later also immigrated to California), the commercial forms most recently connected with "California moderne," for me at least, were in some measure inspired by "Depression moderne."[33] The slic-chic of proto-hi-tech (primarily interior accouterments) 1930's modernity, seen

29.   *Ibid.*, pp. 72-79.

30.   Ellwood reportedly spends a portion of each year in Italy, where his interests have shifted from architecture to art.

31.   *Architecture and Culture, Los Angeles 2*, Architectural Design 52, Academy Editions, 1982, see photograph p. 117.

32.   *Ibid.*, p. 116.

33.   Gebhard and von Breton, *op. cit.*

FIG. 8

FIG. 9

FIG. 10

FIG. 11

FIG. 12

in the work of Kem Weber[34] and J.R. Davidson accomplished a startling scale shift in the 1960's and 1970's when Cesar Pelli was at Victor Gruen's office, Paul Kennon was still in Los Angeles, and Anthony Lumsden established control of design at DMJM's office. Such projects as the Pacific Design Center by Pelli in Los Angeles and the Beverly Hills Project by DMJM (Lumsden) begin to speak of the issues implied here.

The disillusionment of the late 1960's led in L.A. in part to the riots in Watts and in part to the reflections of one's own condition in the mirror glass buildings (metaphorically reminding me of the aimlessness of the heroine in Joan Didion's novel, *Play It As It Lays*). Charles Luckman's office building, Ocean Gate,[35] Lomax/Rock Associates' Neville Office Building in Santa Monica (Fig. 8) and their Rodeo Corner project in Beverly Hills (1982) (Fig. 9) all address the subject of the taut skin membrane more than they convey interests in expanding upon the several regional traditions well known to us all. Of course, the exaggerations common to *The California Condition* (and its Hollywood outpost) suggest such exercises. Even the Beverly Center project in West Hollywood by Welton Becket Associates (Fig. 10), while presumably elaborating upon that side of Pelli's Pacific Design Center (the circulation system as a means of expression), inadvertently conveys the general hermeticism common to the Pelli project (internalization as a programmatic constraint, externalized).

Extrusion (functional and spatial eccentricity suppressed in favor of an overriding generalized form) remains the name of the game for most of those mentioned above, perhaps as a way of conveying the mobility connected with California's notorious freeway system. But it is not by any means the only commercial game in town for architects attempting to transmute modernist canons into California's capitalist world. The San Francisco office of Skidmore, Owings and Merrill, generally, and Marc Goldstein, particularly,[36] modify these extrusion techniques, establishing a kind of architecture suitable at the ground plane to "pedestrian scale." Goldstein's 333 California Street project in San Francisco (Fig. 11) and his Crocker Center project in Los Angeles (Fig. 12) are examples of this humanizing device. More generalized, these projects are somewhat less categorizable than those mentioned earlier. More interesting are the new

34.   David Gebhard and Harriette von Breton, *Kem Weber The Moderne in Southern California 1920-1941*, (The Art Galleries, University of California, Santa Barbara, 1969).

35.   *Architecture and Culture, Los Angeles 2*, Architectural Design 52, Academy Editions, 1982, p. 99.

36.   Partner in Charge of Design, San Francisco office, Skidmore, Owings and Merrill.

FIG. 13

condominium towers of Jon Thogmartin (Fig. 13), an early 1980's arrival in Santa Monica, whose tall towers show a possible new direction for the large-scale structure. In certain ways this project reflects both post-L.A. Pelli projects, the Houston Galleria housing and the New York Battery Park Office Complex.

MANIPULATED MATERIALISM

The first sub-section connected with *Manipulated Materialism* predictably deals with the pragmatism inherent in both commercial buildings and housing. As we have seen in the previous section, the large-scale commercial structure in California has made a (dubious) name for itself in its extruded reflective image on the landscape. Housing, however, also pragmatically addressed by California architects, benefits (or suffers, depending on your point of view) from no such coalescence.

Multi-family housing has simply been built — consciously, attractively, even sometimes wonderfully, but never didactically — operating at a high, but never brilliant, level. Evolving in some measure as a product of a beach-front, wind-surfing mentality, California housing has nonetheless been imported by the rest of the United States in mass quantities — partially in envy, partially in jest, but imported all the same — attractive solutions for an amenity-craving culture. Such architects as Marquis /Stoller, Ray Kappe and Fisher/Friedman (and even, when pressed, William Turnbull, Jr.) have responded to post-World War II housing needs in California with a vengeance. The most recent resident architect in this category is Rob Quigley, whose San Diego practice includes such projects as Pacifica Townhomes at Point Loma.[37] Not necessarily remarkable in itself,[38] it nonetheless has a handsome quality common to his antecedents. (Fig. 14) It is curious and a bit disappointing that a state whose architects have a tradition of responding to the idiosyncratic could not produce an alternative as compelling as the now-familiar "marketing" imperative. Indeed, it is the marketing aspect of Southern California architecture that is worth dwelling upon for a bit, but not in housing.

With capitalism, multi-family housing can be construed as an effect, not a cause. The marketplace itself often establishes the way in which major products such as housing absorb much of the rest of American material production. The proposed shopping mall in San Diego by John Jerde is an interesting case in point. Designed to appeal to a diverse market —

FIG. 14

37.   *Progressive Architecture*, vol. LXIII, no. 3 (March 1982), pp. 92-94.

38.   Quigley's relief drawings and models reflect optimism in their brilliant colors representing the spirit of the place.

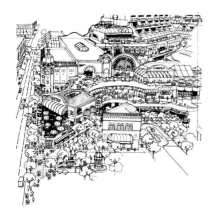

FIG. 15

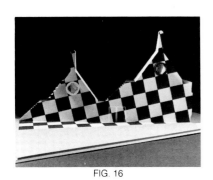

FIG. 16

FIG. 17

Chicanos, sailors, La Jolla gentry, etc. — it employs metaphor to attract (European hill town or portscape, take your pick) (Fig. 15) and projects romantically contrived (or deceptive, if you like) imagery by which it attempts to hawk production. Richard Saul Wurman, a well-known architectural media person, was occasional hype consultant to this extravaganza. Ultimately, I feel, the California marketplace and its mass housing suffer from the blatancy of the most direct form of capitalism — the hard sell.

In the world of *Manipulated Materialism* it is a short step from the marketplace to the contorted forms often connected with the *agony* attributed to Hollywood. If there is a recent architectural father-figure in this area, I would suggest that it is Thomas Vreeland, Jr. It is confirmed by his attempts at coalescing disparate architectural persons under the rubric of "The Silvers," a term which designates architects, especially in California, interested in extrusion and in reflective surfaces (Pelli and Lumsden, for example). Tim Vreeland's leadership at UCLA and his indiscriminate support of the broadest possible range of young, up-beat faculty types qualify him for this dubious distinction.

While many architects have been employed by those involved with the movie industry, not all have formally responded by producing architecture work-in-kind. But there now seems to be a tendency among some current practitioners to produce work that is at once cutting edge and, frankly, just off-the-wall. The architect most obviously displaying these disparate qualities is Eric Owen Moss. Surprisingly, his apprenticeship includes a tour of duty with Paffard Clay, one of the most humorless of recent practitioners. Yet Moss, perhaps when he was released from Clay's strident constructivism, produced projects that, for me, have such dubious progenitors as Johnie's Coffeeshop on the Wilshire Miracle Mile (1962).[39] Both in his San Fernando Valley Fun House (Fig. 16) project and in his wonderful just completed Petal House addition in West Los Angeles (Fig. 17), Moss plows new ground in the not-yet-legitimate area of "ironic architecture." A brilliant, if eccentric craftsman, Moss' notorious Pinball House (with James Stafford) paved the way in a direction that has several advocates — again, the presence of *The California Condition.*

An even more bizarre version of architect-gone-Hollywood is the case of Michael Franklin Ross. A "Rowe clone"[40] gone west, Ross worked at the

39.   Banham, *op. cit.,* p. 199.

40.   A disarmingly accurate way of describing those architectural alumni both of Cornell and the brilliant architect/theoretician, Colin Rowe, who produced an entire generation of jargon-spouting, formal manipulators from coast to coast.

FIG. 18

FIG. 19

FIG. 20

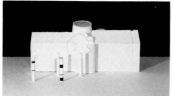

FIG. 21

FIG. 22

FIG. 23

feet of Anthony Lumsden at DMJM. (I don't think there's a more appropriate way to describe a Lumsden apprenticeship.) Having completed his popular (if not particularly intellectual *Post Metabolism* book), Ross now has his own practice in Santa Monica, where his recently completed office project (Fig. 18) attracts the eye far more than do the self-consciously stylized drawings produced under his direction. Encouragingly, his Peter Greenberg House addition in Sherman Oaks (Fig. 19), a backyard residential extension, refreshingly returns to earlier, indigenous California forms so calming for the innocent viewer. A similar project by the Solana Beach architects, Batter/Kay, for the Warren Beach House (Fig. 20) is another example of current interest in formal manipulation — in this case quite exquisitely contrived. Another example of this trend is demonstrated by the 1982 Altenau Residence (Fig. 21) by Martinez/Wong, where the formally idiosyncratic becomes the norm — *The California Condition.* Before "upping the ante" on formal manipulation, it is necessary to mention in passing the work of Eugene Kupper in this context. A bit too young to be labeled a "brilliant eccentric," I can think of no other fitting title for this fascinating architect whose Nilsson House in Bel Air[41] blends many of the California traditions thus far described.

The final sub-section herein is by definition the most bizarre. It is as close as I wish to come to describing such zinging trends as New Wave, Punk and Attitude. Through the use of irony,[42] ambiguity and alienation (a torturous triumvirate if there ever was 1 . . . 2 . . . 3!!!), these architects argue the case of contemporaneity. An example of curiosities within this category might be Richard Fernau's not-so-recent (but clearly wonderful) Franks for the Memories fast food restaurant at the base of an office building in San Francisco. Of note here is the spectacularly talented young Oakland firm called Ace Architects. With respect to Attitude, whose character is the use of unexpected juxtapositions, Ace writes: "A house is much more revealing (and interesting) when it's not just a house; better if it's a theatre, an ocean liner, maybe an artichoke. It is with the discovery of the right mix of corollaries that design begins."[43] With their Hieroglyph Building (Fig. 22) and their Figaro project (Fig. 23), both in Oakland, the work of this young, ambitiously gifted firm suggests extraordinary possibilities inherent in the new amalgam.

The Retirement Beach House at San Elijo State Park by Martinez/Wong

41.   Biennale di Venezia, *op. cit.*, see photograph pp. 222-223.

42.   See *New York Magazine*, vol. 15, no. 29 (July 26, 1982), pp. 24-32.

43.   Letter to author, dated June 8, 1982.

FIG. 24

FIG. 25

FIG. 26

FIG. 27

(Fig. 24) juxtaposes disparate forms on the surface of a "wall" house without attempting either reconciliation or resolution — a particularly apt approach for the post-H Bomb set. Performance art as architecture can be said to be the domain of the self-styled, unwashed San Diegan, Thomas Grondona, whose Zanzibar remodeling project (Fig. 25), by revealing what is apparently the project's original form, allows the new to be measured against the old without prejudice. Finally, the practice of Ted Smith includes a particularly appealing theory that he calls "Blendo." In Smith's Nelson Corner House project (Fig. 26), for example, facades adjacent to each corner reflect each of their respective neighbors (Fig. 27): it is as if the presence of the house itself is denied — the ultimate in "concealed contextualism."

THE DEMATERIALIZED (DISAPPEARING?) CUTTING EDGE

There is an entirely new phenomenon beginning to make its presence felt all over California — Dematerialization. It is being approached in two fundamentally different ways: 1) reductivist thought based on attitudes emanating from neo-Marxist theoreticians, significantly at work in Europe, and 2) the conceptual abstractionists whose work derives in large measure from being in proximity to some of America's most avant-garde 1980's artists.

The former group, primarily based in Northern California, produces architectural drawings and even, on occasion, buildings not dissimilar to those of Mario Botta and Aldo Rossi, though it is difficult to imagine just how the Bay Area resembles either the Ticino Canton in Switzerland or the Veneto in Northern Italy. Nonetheless, the formal similarities between Botta and Rossi, and, for example, Andrew Batey and Marc Mack cannot go unmentioned. Batey and Mack's several projects displayed at the 1980 Venice Biennale,[44] for example, contain not only the symbols of classical antiquity but signs of empty European granaries as well as the vacuity associated with Rossi's cemetery project at Modena, Italy. Lars Lerup's "Analogies for the Drywall" project of 1978, exhibited at the Philippe Bonnafont Gallery in San Francisco (1981),[45] poetically reveal architectural possibilities inherent in what de-constructionists call the silence of language, i.e., jargon for "primal essentiality." Today's architectural generation is only too aware of the condition of what Peter Eisenman calls

44.   Biennale di Venezia, op. cit., see photograph pp. 81-83.

45.   Some of the drawings from that exhibition are in the author's collection and are therefore familiar to him.

"imminence," i.e., living with the threat of nuclear destruction. An excellent example of architects' building within the self-imposed constraints of cultural annihilation is the group known simply as Morphosis — Michael Rotondi and Thom Mayne. In their 2-4-6-8 House in Venice,[46] using reductive and inexpensive materials, Morphosis alludes to an essential way of life seldom seen except for farm buildings in Northern Italy. By addressing existential facts intrinsic to their reductive architecture they open up possibilities not generally considered by contemporary American architects. In their hands post-functionalism begins to look quite compelling.

Finally, inescapably, one comes both to the *oeuvre* and the persona of Frank O. Gehry. A brilliant "California schizophrenic," Frank Gehry has had one of the most astonishingly influential careers in architecture in America. His wide-ranging career has embraced pragmatic housing, off-the-wall corrugated cardboard furniture, constructional fragments and perspectival distortions. His well-known associations with Southern California artists such as Chuck Arnoldi, Sam Francis, Ed Ruscha, Ron Davis, etc., have given him the perspective to continue his own personal formal and cultural investigations into the conceptual architecture of the early 1980's. They have also placed him, willingly or not, into a position of leadership for a "now" generation of architects, often unwilling to look backward over their shoulders. It is important here to acknowledge that I approach the subject of Frank Gehry without Socratic distance since his influence and friendship have often been directed my way. More than that, it is not possible in an essay of this brevity to seriously deal with Gehry as "having evolved a relaxed, highly personal style, evocative of, and with an affinity for, the idiosyncratic in American taste-culture."[47] (Olivier Boissiere's recent book tells all.[48])

Craig Hodgetts and Robert Mangurian of Studio Works are in the Gehry mold as they continue to produce evocative, drawn images of America seen in a perspective opposite to the one Saul Steinberg originally intended. Hodgetts' drawings for the international exhibition entitled *American Architectural Alternatives* are at a conceptual pitch normally not

46. *Progressive Architecture*, vol. LXIII, no. 3 (March, 1982), pp. 80-83.

47. Morris Lesser, "Is Romanticism Alive and Well and Living in America?", *American Architectural Alternatives, an International Exhibition* (Uno Art Gallery, Omaha, Nebraska, 1980), inside cover.

48. Oliver Boissiere, *Gehry Site Tigerman, Trois Portraits de l'artiste en architecte* (Editions du Moniteur, Paris, France, 1981), pp. 12-59.

49. See no. 47 above.

FIG. 28

FIG. 29

FIG. 30

attached to architectural production. This is true as well of Roland Coate (the artist, not the architect) and Coy Howard. Howard, at least, is attempting to transfer his particular brand of conceptual prowess into the physical fact of architecture. His recent Gross Residence in Hollywood[49] (Fig. 28) is an attempt at hybridization without synthetic resolution. Another architect operating at a primarily conceptual level is Frederick Fisher, whose fragmentation owes, it seems to me, a considerable debt to Gehry as well. Fisher's Jorgensen Residence project (1980-82) (Fig. 29) polygonally juxtaposes walls much in the way many of Gehry's projects do. Frank Israel's current projects also demonstrate a considerable conceptual debt to Gehry, while nonetheless also revealing Israel's own series of self-discoveries. His Liberty Tower fashion photographic apartment remodeling in New York City (1982) (Fig. 30) is a brilliant study in dematerialized essentiality.

Would that there were a Hegelian way to conclude such a wide-ranging essay. It is impossible to predict where either California or its architects will go — but that's the fortunate part of anything to do with California. Luckily enough for us all, it continues to be more the laboratory than the battleground on which American mores are evaluated both in conceptual as well as actualized terms. These architects and their own eccentricities are more often a funnel than a sieve through which America pours its heart.

Stanley Tigerman, Chicago
August 1982

ILLUSTRATIONS

CALIFORNIA ARCHITECTURE — CELEBRATIONS AND INNOVATIONS

A group of risk-taking, rule-breaking, inventive and innovative architects is creating a new architecture in California today. Pluralism has superseded the minimalism that prevailed in California architecture into the mid-1970's. A consequence of this lean, spare style, with some exceptions,[1] was that the high-art California architect felt limited — boxed in by an aesthetic of reductionism. Design exploration had nowhere to go.

The box, which came in three varieties, had become the problem. In addition to the ubiquitous neutral stucco box, there were the steel and glass boxes created for John Entenza's distinguished Case Study House Program, which continued into the early 1960's[2]. Instead of serving as a prototype for industrial mass production (It never happened!), these skinny, steel-frame houses spoke of a Spartan simplicity that had little appeal to the local clientele. The style had been refined to such a degree that it could not be developed any further. As for the local Angelenos, it left them cold, as Reyner Banham commented so well:

> The very puritanism and understatement that we admire in the Case Study style make it an unlikely starter in the cultural ambience of Los Angeles — or rather, make it an unlikely finisher. The permissive atmosphere means that almost anything can be started; what one doubts is that there was enough flesh on these elegant bones to satisfy local tastes for long.[3]

That this was indeed the case is evidenced by author John Chase's fascinating research into the metamorphoses of California's neutral boxes by the remodelings of decorators and builders. His description of the fate of Case Study House No. 17, designed and built by Craig Ellwood in 1956, illustrates the clients' rejection of the style that architects would soon rebel against themselves:

> Although the original client had some doubtful moments about the house, and the manner in which it was to be furnished, such as the steel and glass and the hard beds and coconut chairs, a later owner had no such doubts. John Woolf and his adopted son Robert Koch Woolf knew they didn't like the finishes of the house they had purchased and proceeded to rip them out. 'They remodeled the house in 1962 by opening up the center and by adding Doric columns over the steel uprights, in order to

1.   John Lautner; Callister, Payne and Bischoff; Valentino Agnoli and John Marsh Davis are notable exceptions. See also David Gebhard and Susan King, *A View of California Architecture, 1960-1976* (San Francisco Museum of Modern Art, San Francisco, 1977).

2.   Esther McCoy, *Modern California Houses: 1945-1962* (Reinhold Publishing Corp., New York, 1962).

3.   Reyner Banham, *Los Angeles: The Architecture of Four Ecologies* (Pelican Books, Harmondsworth, England, 1973), p. 230.

give this beautifully made contemporaneous building a patina of age.' . . .

Was the result successful? *House Beautiful* had no reservations about this remodel job. 'In the enchanted hour of dusk, one might be reliving the past in a columned villa of Basae or among the temples of Paestum.'[4]

This blatant disregard of traditional notions of architectural integrity illustrates how both the profession and the public reacted against the reductive minimalism of both clean-cut stucco boxes and steel and glass ice cubes. After all, in 1962, the year of this remodel, which was only one among hundreds, Charles Moore, who with Robert Venturi was one of the co-founders of the post-modernist movement, was building his highly influential house in Orinda, California. The unorthodox attitudes of Charles Moore were so new to elder modernist Gregory Ain, that when Ain first confronted Moore's Orinda House he thought it French Provincial.

Quite unintentionally, it was the richly inventive Moore himself, who, with Bill Turnbull (MLTW), provided the third box form that would prove a design straitjacket for the California, and, as well, the national architect. The vertical shed roof, box form of Condominium No. 1 at Sea Ranch was based on local building vernacular, "the straightforwardly utilitarian wood frame building of the mining and boom towns of the second half of the 19th century."[5] As New York Times architecture critic Paul Goldberger pointed out, "Many distinguished works of architecture have not proved a good model. The crisp diagonals of its shed roofs were all too easy to copy cheaply, and by the end of the decade a kind of 'rustic modern' had already become a tired cliche."[6] Sea Ranch, like the landmark Case Study House, became an architectural dead end as well.

The formularization of California architecture, along with an international disenchantment with the canonical stance of modernism and the publication of Robert Venturi's book *Complexity and Contradiction in Architecture*, which advocated new architectural attitudes, coupled with the flamboyance of California's pop consumerist culture, helped set the stage for a new California architecture.

Although many local, national and international architects have had strong influences on the current course of West Coast architecture, the two figures who repeatedly dominate most serious discussions of California

4.   John Chase, *Exterior Decoration* (Hennessey and Ingalls, Los Angeles, 1982). Chase quotes from *House Beautiful*, vol. 103, no. 9 (September 1965), in the first instance pp. 134-141 and in the second p. 14.

5.   John Beach, "The Bay Area Tradition: 1890-1918," *Bay Area Houses*, Sally Woodbridge, ed. (Oxford University Press, New York, 1976), p. 23.

6.   *House Beautiful*, vol. 124, no. 9 (May 1982), pp. 104, 105 and 153.

architecture are Charles Moore and Frank O. Gehry.

Charles Moore's tenure as a California-influenced and California-influencing architect is a long one, going back thirty-five years. Of his early days in California, he says,

> I got my first job in San Francisco in 1947. There, the wildest and most wonderful work belonged to the past. Bernard Maybeck and other splendidly crazy people were still very much alive in 1947. The Greene Brothers were among us, and the work of Willis Polk. There were a lot of shingle fantasies, very Beaux Arts. In northern California, there was still a sort of more or less controlled goofiness in the Bay region . . . altogether crazy in a wonderful way.[7]

It was almost as if Maybeck's independence skipped a generation, one that Moore calls the "sensible" generation, and the tradition passed directly from Maybeck to Moore. Moore relates, "Maybeck said that the rules which might obtain elsewhere didn't really obtain in California."[8]

From the seminal Sea Ranch and Orinda House in Northern California to the sensuous Southern California Burns House and Moore's own condominium in Los Angeles — and, of course, the Piazza d'Italia in New Orleans — the Moore influence has become pervasive. His own highly eclectic, personal brand of California independence, full of imagery and whimsy, remains unrestrained by rules. Moore has said, "As an absorber of images and influences, I operate between the soaking action of a sponge and the gulps of a piranha."[9]

He has taught the California architect (and a world community of appreciative architects) to be *inclusive* of shapes, colors, forms, memories, hopes, dreams and desires. He has taught that the most ordinary and mundane acts may be elevated to meaningful events; even the everyday act of taking a bath can be a special moment, as in his historicizing fourposter-canopied, aedicula-enclosed bathtub in his house in Orinda (1962). In California's narcissistic society, these ideas take on added meaning. To Moore's way of thinking, "Rescuing the everyday from humdrum oblivion," is a noble cause.[10] Moore disagrees with those who respond with horror to an architecture of wider sources, who feel it will mean, "unbridled license, lowered discipline, bad stuff." He thinks, "It is

7.   John W. Cook and Heinrich Klatz, "Charles Moore," *Conversations With Architects* (Praeger Publications, New York, 1973), p. 232.

8.   *Ibid.*, p. 233.

9.   Charles W. Moore, "Personal Statement," *The Work of Charles W. Moore, Architecture and Urbanism*, vol. 92 (Tokyo, 1978), p. 7.

10.   *Ibid.*, p. 6.

only reasonable to press hard for using, without fear and shame, the riches of the world at hand."[11]

This attitude applies especially to architectural history, whether real or imagined. Moore's legacy from Maybeck and Polk is the unabashed historicism that pervades his most recent work. Although sometimes criticized, this historicism establishes a cultural base, a connection with past generations that Moore deems important to the 1980's.

Architectural historian David Gebhard of the University of California, Santa Barbara, calls California historicism, and more specifically Moore's historicism, a "fairy tale historicism."[12] He observes,

> The one aspect of California's approach to history which strikingly sets it off from Europe and much of the United States is its open lack of seriousness. The California tradition of history (i.e. especially its own history) lies in the world of the child and the constuct of the 'fairy tale.'[13]

Moore's use of history in his buildings and in his writings has a gentle, playful charm which draws one in, as in the make-believe world of a young child.[14]

The other dominant figure in current California architecture, Frank Gehry, has, like Moore, set out to establish a no-rules architecture. He has said,

> I try to rid myself, and the other members of the firm, of the burden of culture and look for new ways to approach the work. I want to be open-ended. There are no rules, no right or wrong. I am confused as to what's ugly and what's pretty. Buildings become obsolete, so individual criteria are not the issue. I think an architect should respond to the site and budget, but be allowed to create space that is flexible.[15]

If Moore can be thought of as comfortable, whimsical, and picturesque, substitute words like ugly, ambiguous, experimental, sculptural and process-oriented for Gehry. Gehry has enumerated his dominant concerns as "cheapness, destruction, distortion, illusion, layering and surrealism."[16] There is nothing pretty about Gehry's architecture, yet it has a compelling strength and uncompromising dedication and seriousness that has given

11.   *Ibid.*, p. 11.

12.   David Gebhard, "Charles Moore and the West Coast," *The Work of Charles W. Moore, Architecture and Urbanism*, vol. 92 (Tokyo, 1978), p. 48.

13.   *Loc. cit.*.

14.   *Loc. cit.*.

15.   Introduction to lecture "Frank Gehry: The Search for A 'No Rules' Architecture," Harvard Graduate School of Design, November 29, 1979.

16.   Martin Filler, "Eccentric Space: Frank Gehry," *Art in America*, vol. 68, no. 6 (June 1980), p. 114.

him a leadership position not only in California but internationally as well.

To Gehry architecture is an art, but an art that must always serve his clients' needs. His close contacts with and mutual appreciation of various artists' work has led him to incorporate some of their concerns in his work, especially explorations into the natures of process, materials, and perception, in particular forced perspective.

The building process — unfinished wood frames, exposed studs — has an inherent beauty to Gehry. It was Gehry's remodeling of a "dumb and ordinary" pink bungalow for himself in Santa Monica that gave full expression to this involvement with process. Plaster was removed to expose lath slats and framing was left unfinished. The results, at first startling, have earned Gehry the reputation as an "architect's architect." Taking process one step further, Gehry has elevated his architectural striptease one step further by employing one of his most compelling devices. That is to expose studs and encase them like jewels between layers of glass.

Gehry's unequivocal acceptance of context has inspired a new generation of California architects. His acceptance and exploration of many of the ticky-tacky materials of vernacular and high-tech architecture of the Sun Belt cities in general and Southern California specifically — corrugated steel, chain link fences, wire-mesh safety glass, cardboard, sheets of unfinished exterior plywood, green asphalt shingles, siding and exposed concrete blocks — are characteristics of his work now found in the work of many other architects in Southern California. But Gehry's way of using these materials is uniquely his. Like a sculptor, he attacks each material, explores its abilities to produce desired results, discovers any hidden potential. Then he might finish with it and go on to another material.

His latest exploration is post-modernism. He is examining it and re-examining it much the way that he delved into the qualities of chain link:

> I go where my explorations take me — I never go back. I never turn off the searching until, like a mathematician, I've solved the problem. When faced with a new problem to explore I feel like a curious cat who has been given the freedom to play. I feel like a voyeur.[17]

Gehry has the same attitude toward style. Trained as a modernist, he was at the forefront of breaking its rigid dogma. Coincidentally, one of the final flowerings of the neutral stucco box was Gehry's 1964 Danziger studio for a graphic artist, an abstract composition of two discrete geometric forms.

---

17.   From an interview with Frank Gehry by the author on August 3, 1982.

Ironically, it was this abstract, sculptural work that brought Gehry to the attention of the Los Angeles art community, including Ed Moses, Ron Davis, Chuck Arnoldi, Larry Bell, and Billy Al Bengston. From interaction and dialogue with these artists his work veered dramatically away from modernistic abstraction.

As Gehry's work has matured and he has attained the recognition he so much deserves within architectural circles, he is now interacting with the architectural community. The Wosk addition reflects probings into the forms of post-modernism. In addition, it mirrors other concerns as well, primarily Gehry's sensitivity to a client's familiarity with the latest in the contemporary art scene. Although he sometimes fears that his "hands-on" approach may have become too concerned with creating art objects, it is unlikely that he will settle on a fixed architectural vocabulary. The need for exploration seems to be at the very heart of Gehry's psyche.

With all that has happened and is happening in California architecture, no one style has emerged, and no coherent group of practitioners has emerged (although Frank Gehry's followers are sometimes seen as a group, especially by the European and Japanese press).

There is definitely a dividing line between Northern and Southern California: San Francisco is more urban, more traditional, and with a long tradition of wood building, while Southern California, with its stucco tradition, has always been more of a barometer of pop culture. Herewith some very brief observations on characteristics noted in the work from the three cities included in the show.

SAN DIEGO

San Diego architecture is characterized by its vitality, its freedom and its ability to take very seriously Charles Moore's advice about not being overly serious. In fact, the influences of both Moore and Gehry can clearly be seen in the work of Rob Quigley, Tom Grondona and Ted Smith.

These three architects often speak of the joy, the delight and the ability to create a sense of place that they have learned from Moore. From Gehry there is an openness to experimentation with materials, ideas, even divergent aesthetics. And from both masters they have learned to respond to both the clients' needs and the existing context. Building realities like economics, context and clients' dreams are paramount concerns to these three San Diegans. With all the apparent fun and games, this group of architects is reality-based. Don't let all the talk about surfing fool you.

Although part artist/part architect, Tom Grondona approaches each job with an elaborate program study book to be filled out by clients. Shapes, materials, colors, forms might mix in the most exuberant way, yet, like his other San Diego colleagues, Grondona has a firm interest in meeting budgets and fulfilling needs.

Ted Smith has recently dealt with the realities of "spec" building in the creation of three deceivingly simple boxes that blend the realities of the market place with high architecture. Smith has come up with the term BLENDO to describe the stylistic merging of the dreams of several neighbors' houses into one new house. To smooth out the ugly transitions that occur when a new work of architecture must be built between existing buildings, Smith borrows from all, creating a new transitional style. Yet to garner the widest possible appeal for his spec houses, he has left the interiors as open and flexible as possible.

Quigley's recently completed Forecast Condominium juxtaposes tract house details against symbolic references to 1920's bungalow courts and hard-edge materials against 1950's patios, all behind a facade of 1940's clapboard.

When you ask a San Diego architect about his design sources, he'll usually point to a house down the street.

LOS ANGELES

Los Angeles architects are the current favorites of the international press. Although their intentions remain serious, one can't help but wonder if all this fanfare from the press is a bit premature. On the other hand, Los Angeles architects are likely to be up on the latest architectural news — whether it is a building by European rationalists or the work of, say, Isozaki. The annual arrival of architecture critic Charles Jencks helps to keep this international interchange alive and lively.

Frank Gehry's gift to these Los Angeles architects is that he has taught them to get outside the conventional formalism of architecture. This has given them a sense of freedom and an ability to explore what he has already initiated. Of these Los Angeles architects the works of Craig Hodgetts, Bob Mangurian, Coy Howard, Morphosis and Eric Moss stand out. Moss's experiments with flat, two-dimensional pattern and three-dimensional form and his flower-form, Petal House are especially refreshing.

SAN FRANCISCO

If San Diego architects are looking around the corner, and Los Angeles architects are scanning the latest issues of *Progressive Architecture* or *Domus*, then San Francisco architects are likely to be looking back to Palladio or Art Deco structures or the wood vernacular structures of the turn-of-the-century. A sense of the past dominates this group of architects (who are, incidentally, more pictorial and less model oriented than their southern neighbors).

Thomas Gordon Smith claims that his passion is more for the elements of architecture available throughout history than for the past per se. A more synthesized use of classical architectural elements can be seen in the house he is currently building for himself and his family. But never doubt for a moment that Smith is anything less than a card-carrying Californian. Maybeck remains an important influence on his work.

Very much a product of the Bay Area tradition, Bill Turnbull shares many of the concerns of Charles Moore. In fact, when Moore and Turnbull associate, to this day the results are generally more disciplined, better detailed, more carefully thought out than when Moore works alone. Turnbull's Fisher Winery is a building with a strong debt to the vernacular tradition, but it has a strength and unity of purpose that make it totally original.

Barbara Stauffacher-Solomon and Dan Solomon link the house to the garden and the town. Regaining paradise lost is Stauffacher's goal and she envisions it via a series of public and semi-private gardens. Her exquisitely beautiful drawings portray her feelings of a garden as hallowed ground. "A square of grass is a garden. A tree is a garden. We plot a path, enclose a lawn, order trees and make the water rise. We make a park; a green theatre for playing and play-acting."[18]

Where is California going? What is its future? Stauffacher and Solomon provide one answer:

> In California, we now stand at a peculiar point. It is quite within our hands to decide whether or not we shall have a history. Perhaps it is the *genius loci* of California to be perpetually new. Some people in Los Angeles think this is so, that the best process, and one which captures the essence of the place, is one which obliterates obsolescence in a present of eternally gleaming novelty. To us, this argument seems unconvincing. California is characterized by a most condensed form of cultural history, and the present seems always to be redolent with nostalgia for the very recent, but impossibly remote and exotic past. In the best of music, cars, hair styles, clothes, and architecture, history is an element of hipness. These works of architecture and planning are about the self-conscious retention of the past in a process of rapid an radical changes.[19]

Past, present, future — where is California architecture going and how will the architectural forms of the past and present combine to create an

18.   Extracted from Daniel Solomon and Barbara Stauffacher-Solomon's philosophical statement elsewhere in this catalogue.

19.   *Ibid.*

architecture for the future? For those who view pluralism as a positive note, the present atmosphere is both a healthy one and a rich one. Current California attitudes have produced an architecture that constantly renews itself, infused with new and old-new sources, rather than an architecture that feeds on itself, reaching an inevitable dead end. All balls are in the air, so to speak.

At the moment, the straitjacket of a single style is a danger that does not have to be faced, although the possibility of such a style might be on the horizon. That style is coming to California via the influence of such European neo-rationalists as Aldo Rossi, Leon Krier and Rem Koolhaas.

The style is one that is austere, primitive and based on archetypal forms. A relationship to fascistic architecture has been noted but always denied. The Californians whose work reflects this influence to a varying degree are Batey and Mack, Studio Works (Hodgetts and Mangurian), Morphosis, Coy Howard, Daniel Solomon and Barbara Stauffacher-Solomon. This is an architecture of stark beauty but one wonders as did Reyner Banham when discussing the demise of Case Study Houses, if there is enough "flesh on these elegant bones to satisfy local tastes for long . . . "[20]

The current mood of experimentation and innovation seems to be California's special gift to the architectural scene. That course should be pursued.

Susan Grant Lewin
September 1982

20.   Banham, *loc. cit.*

FRANK O. GEHRY

Principal in the firm of Frank O. Gehry and Associates, Inc., Gehry received his B.Arch. from the University of Southern California and pursued graduate study in City Planning at Harvard University. His drawings and furniture have been exhibited at the Museum of Modern Art, the Cooper Hewitt Museum, and the Louvre. He was elected to the College of Fellows of the American Institute of Architects in 1974. His work has been published extensively in such journals as *Progressive Architecture, Art in America, Architectural Record* and *Time.*

I was recently asked to consider how my uses of space, shape, volume and light address the humanistic as well as socio-political imperatives inherent in the art of architecture. Because of the recent interest shown in the work of Michael Graves, Robert Venturi, Charles Moore, myself and others, I feel the need to acknowledge the issue as fundamental to the acceptance, longevity and possibilities for contemporary architecture. More and more our accomplishments will have to be judged in terms of our ability to fulfill the needs of the greater public while not compromising the aesthetic, cultural and historical imperatives of the medium.

Basically, the issue of formal exploration is one of identification (independently of marketplace manipulation, which in no way is inherent to the process of individual expression). That is, what does it take for the individual to see himself more clearly or state his particular reason for being beyond the fundamental realities of breath, sustenance and habitation? Admittedly, architecture must first address questions and problems of function. While accepting this principle as given, I equally recognize that the notable works in any and every medium have always existed on many other levels as well. It is these levels beyond function that not only allow architecture to maximize its possibilities, but also allow a society to use architecture as one of the means by which it expresses individual and collective consciousness. From the moment Eve plucked the apple, mankind has proclaimed the need for individual expression. The individual in his efforts to make his acts of expression purer — that is, more consistent with how he sees himself — opens the door for others to achieve self-understanding. The common denominator between the individual's need for self-expression and collective society's fulfillment of its needs and aspirations is the manipulation of form. In this sense, nothing has fundamentally changed since early man made marks inside a cave. Now, as then, our marks as well as our treatment of space, color and light, are the best means we have for the greatest possibility of revealing, understanding and achieving inherent truths and realities.

(Transcribed and excerpted by Fred Hoffman from conversations with the architect.)

1

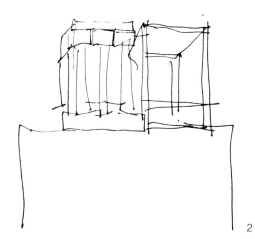

2

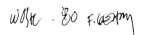
Wolfe · '80 F. Gehry

Wolfe · '81 F. Gehry & Alejo

3

Beverly Hills Residence, Beverly Hills, California 1980-1982

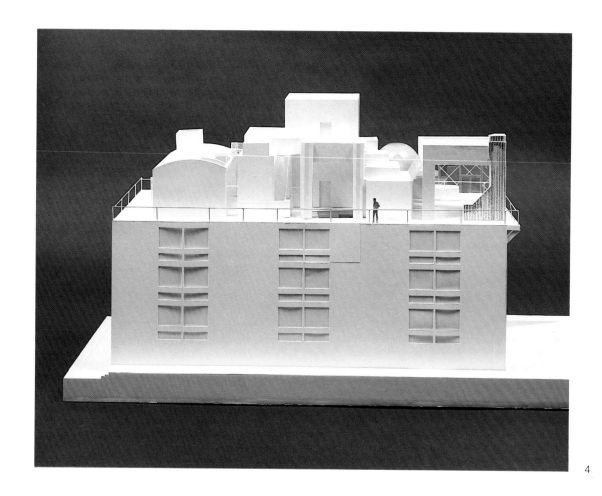

4

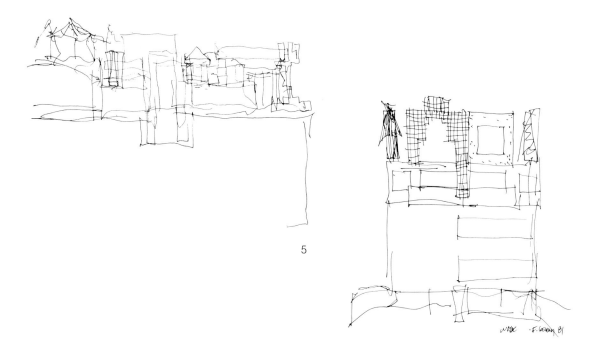

5

Beverly Hills Residence, Beverly Hills, California 1980-1982

6

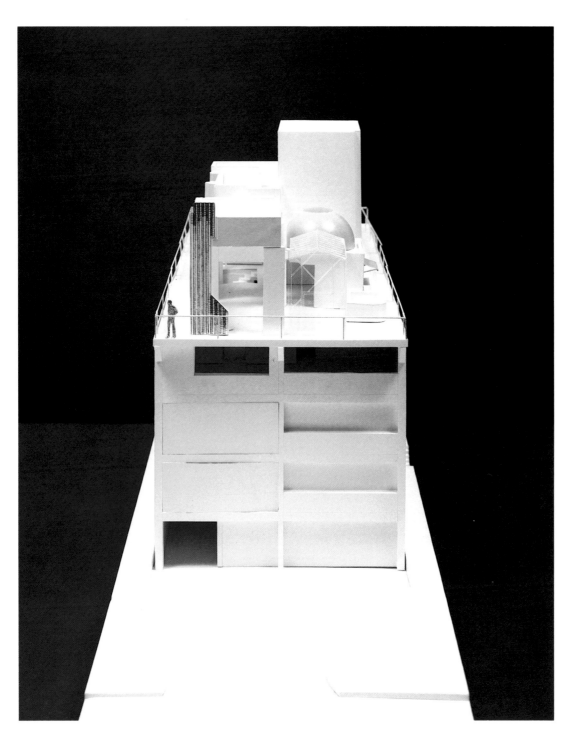

Beverly Hills Residence, Beverly Hills, California 1980-1982

8

The Loyola Law School, Los Angeles, California 1981

9

10

California Aerospace Museum, Venice, California 1982

11

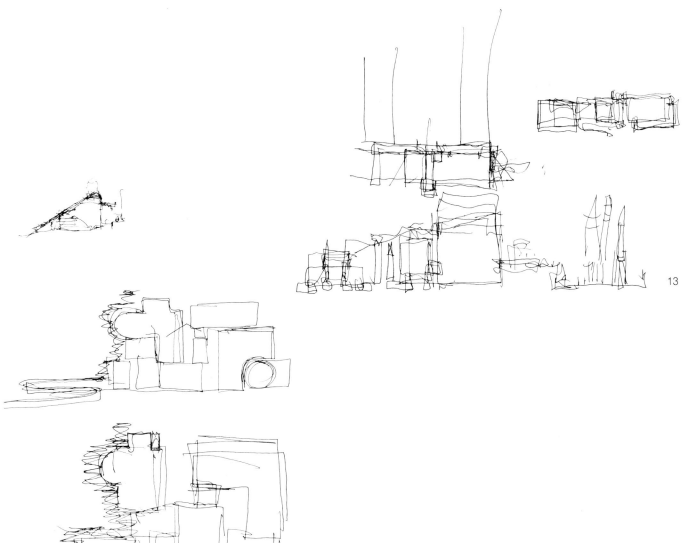

13

12

California Aerospace Museum, Venice, California 1982

TOM GRONDONA

Born in 1950 in San Diego, Grondona received his B.Arch. in 1973 from the Southern California Institute of Architecture. He has studied abroad independently and as an affiliate of California State Poly-Technic University, Pomona. Grondona's work in both architecture and art has received awards and has been exhibited and published extensively. His work has been featured in such publications as *Abitare, Ville Giardini, San Diego Magazine, Home Magazine* (Los Angeles Times) and *San Diego Home/Garden.*

Hello, everybody! I am writing this for the La Jolla Museum of Contemporary Art, which has asked me for a philosophical statement. I've never looked at myself as having a set philosophy, but a mode of attack:

> The site is my canvas,
> the neighborhood, my frame,
> and within the frame,
> my clients,
> squeezed like tubes of paint,
> squirt out their fantasies,
> their dreams and desires.

In Saska's "Star of the Sidewalk"[1] project I was more interested in creating a small urban event than in creating architecture. Saska's restaurant has been here for thirty years and wanted to expand into a building next-door. The problem was that there is a public sidewalk separating the two buildings. The solution came from a fear of creating a restaurant that would compete with itself. Here the lemon of the project became the originator of the concept — one restaurant with a sidewalk as the event going through it. The parade of beach people provides continuous free entertainment for the seated patrons. The main facade (The Yellow Ochre Arch) is recessed 40 feet from the sidewalk to celebrate the small urban space, an outdoor cafe. The project consists of the three major elements of European villages: the Square, the Market, and the Tower (in this case, a borrowed piece of architecture — the elevator shaft of an existing, adjacent condominium, painted blue).

The "Kissing Castles" project took 15 hours from conception to study model. Architecture is a three-dimensional art, which is the way my projects start. Building a study model with little direction opens up avenues of excitement by not being married to any form that grows out of a two-dimensional piece of paper. The creator is free to screw around with the form until he's happy. The first test is to let a scale mock-up evolve from the sketch model by mixing the spontaneity of the study model with the dimension of reality. Of course the ultimate test of my work doesn't stop on the table top. It stops after the bank, the government, the contractor, the client and Father Time have made my baby run the gamuts of their truths.

The last project, "Chateau Explosif," is so hot off the boards I have yet to figure out what I've done ... but then, do I need to?

[1]The title alludes playfully to Anthony's Star of the Sea Room overlooking San Diego Harbor. It is the most elegant unit of a well-known chain of seafood restaurants in San Diego and environs. Saska's site, style and cuisine are typical of an evolved beach front community rather than a developed harbor side. Editor.

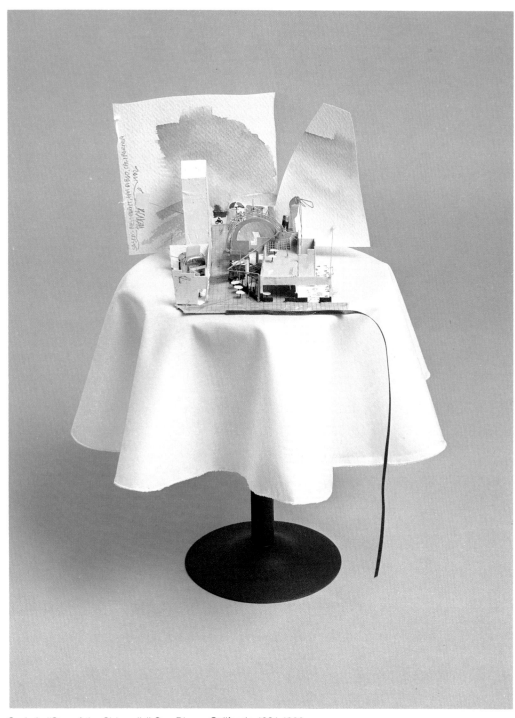

14

Saska's "Star of the Sidewalk," San Diego, California 1981-1982

15

Kissing Castles 1982

16

Project (Château Explosif), Point Loma, California 1982

TOM GRONDONA

FRANK ISRAEL

Born in 1945, Israel received his B.A. in 1967 from the University of Pennsylvania. He attended Yale University and received his M.Arch. in 1971 from Columbia University. He has been a Fellow of the American Academy in Rome (Prix de Rome, 1973-75), and he has worked in Tehran, London, Amsterdam, Rome and New York. Israel currently practices in Santa Monica with Bob Johnson.

So much of what we see around us, so much of today's mainstream, is rooted in the syntax of the past. I certainly cannot turn my back on history. When I lived and practiced in New York, my work endorsed a polemic which challenged the tenets of modernism. In Los Angeles, making architecture demands quick responses to situations that defy the past. The materials and craft of putting materials together borrow from yesterday in a brusque manner. Nothing dictates design parameters when a single family house is constructed adjacent to a twenty-story condominium tower, except the will to do it. And there is nothing particularly coherent or practical about an unpainted plywood wall butting into a piece of glass. What seems natural about this condition is its response to a visual order which embraces so many divergent elements. No other city contains so many choices of habitation with so many topological differences. These choices are reinforced as each one of us goes about his or her business of guiding the physical changes that take place in our *ville d'anges*.

Water was brought down from the mountains to transform the desert into a verdant place, which is now Los Angeles. Each year the city continues to assert itself over the natural world. This does not occur easily. It requires great effort because the land and vegetation are young and continue to change. Driving through Laurel Canyon into Hollywood is like traveling from a wild paradise to an established metropolis. In L.A. this transition takes minutes; in New York it takes hours. Manicured gardens are forever being uprooted, even after careful attention. In New York there is a substructure which is difficult to overturn; nevertheless, when the Westside Highway was abandoned in Lower Manhattan a few years ago, hollyhocks and thistle took over, and the elevated portion of the road became a Babylonian retreat.

As an architect, I aim to enhance the California condition through my work.Juxtaposition is part of the response; camouflage is another. The work I do attempts to establish an armature in which divergent elements interact. They are symbiotic; they do not lose their identies in their struggle to survive. Instead, they become more defined, their edges sharpened. The space which exists between them becomes no less important than the elements themselves.

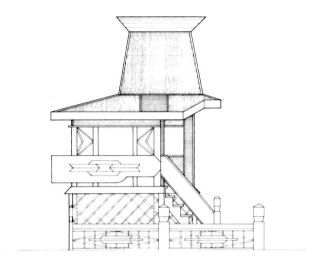

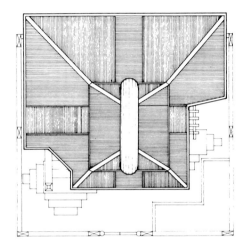

17

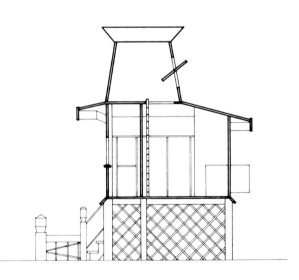

18

Bamboo Bungalows, Manila, Philippines 1980

19

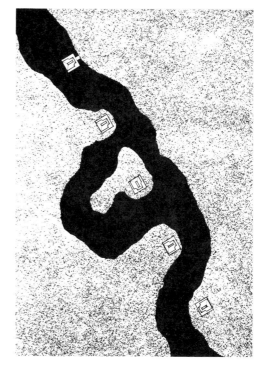

20

Bamboo Bungalows, Manila, Philippines 1980

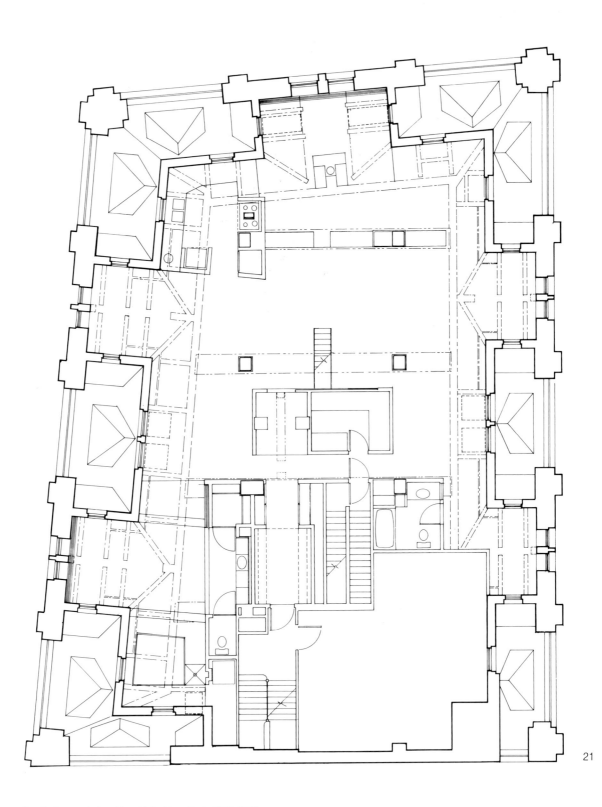

21

Studio for an Artist, New York, New York 1980-1982

Bellisle Ranch, Santa Barbara, California 1980

ANTHONY J. LUMSDEN, FAIA

DANIEL MANN JOHNSON AND MENDENHALL, LOS ANGELES

Lumsden is Principal for Design of the international architectural and engineering firm Daniel Mann Johnson and Mendenhall (DMJM). Lumsden, educated in Australia at the University of Sydney, was elected to the College of Fellows of the American Institute of Architects in 1979. Before joining DMJM in 1964 he was associated with the late Eero Saarinen and with the firm of Kevin Roche/Jonh Dinkeloo and Associates. Lumsden currently serves on the faculty at the University of California, Los Angeles, in the School of Architecture and Urban Design. His work has been featured in numerous professional journals and books.

Changi Hotel, Singapore, Singapore 1980

23

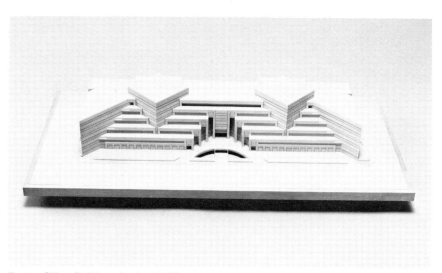

Encino Office Building, Encino, California 1981

24

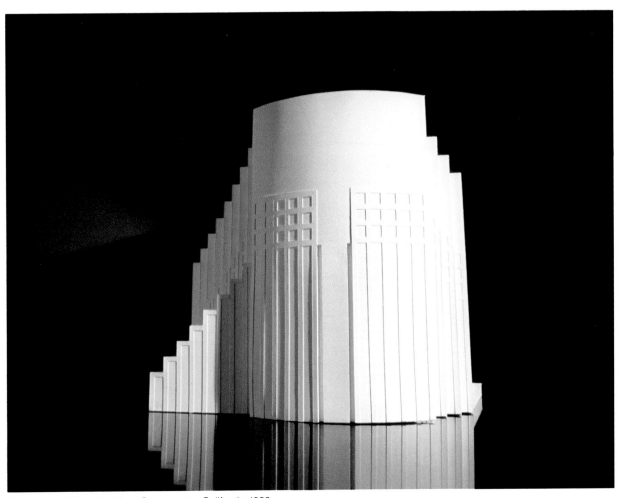

Sacramento Office Building, Sacramento, California 1982

26

Sacramento Office Building, Sacramento, California 1982

27

Knapp Center, Los Angeles, California 1981

29

28

Rahardja Center, Singapore, Singapore 1981

ANTHONY J. LUMSDEN

CHARLES MOORE JOHN RUBLE BUZZ YUDELL

MOORE RUBLE YUDELL, SANTA MONICA

Since our early work such as the Rodes House or a community planning project for Seal Beach we have been fortunate to have clients with strong imagery and vitally held concerns. We have all preferred to work in such situations more than any idealized arrangement of architect-artist with *carte blanche*. This inclination has perhaps been fueled by working in Southern California, a region built on dreams, where the sense of the personal and the possible still seem to thrive.

Having come through a community planning project like the Seal Beach restoration plan with great satisfaction, we found ourselves offering to try the same in designing buildings. St. Matthew's Parish Church, now nearing completion, will be our first such collaborative effort. We are optimistic that such a relationship takes nothing away from the architect but rather gives energy to both parties.

Our interest in clients' participation is a natural extension of our interests in the context and history of any site. While we look to architectural history for cues and inspiration, we hope that our use of history is site and place specific.

In Los Angeles our entry in the Knapp Center Competition refers to an immediate past and place for the making and detailing of a tower on the Miracle Mile. Conventional curtain wall elements are used graphically at base and top to suggest the richly faceted elevations of an earlier Wilshire Boulevard, while the towering palms and globe fountain of the entry court celebrate the broader scale of the street and the slow procession of movement between downtown and the beach. We feel no hesitation in exploring such hybrids, taking cues from multiple sources.

Charles Moore, John Ruble and Buzz Yudell began their joint practice in 1977. Moore, B.Arch., University of Michigan, 1947, M.F.A. and Ph.D., Princeton University, 1956 and 1957, has, in addition to an extensive practice, held numerous faculty positions and co-authored several books. John Ruble received his architectural degrees from the University of California, Los Angeles, and the University of Virginia. His professional experience includes participatory planning and serving as Urban Designer in the Peace Corps (Tunisia). Buzz Yudell received his M.Arch. from Yale University. His work and writing have been published in numerous journals and books.

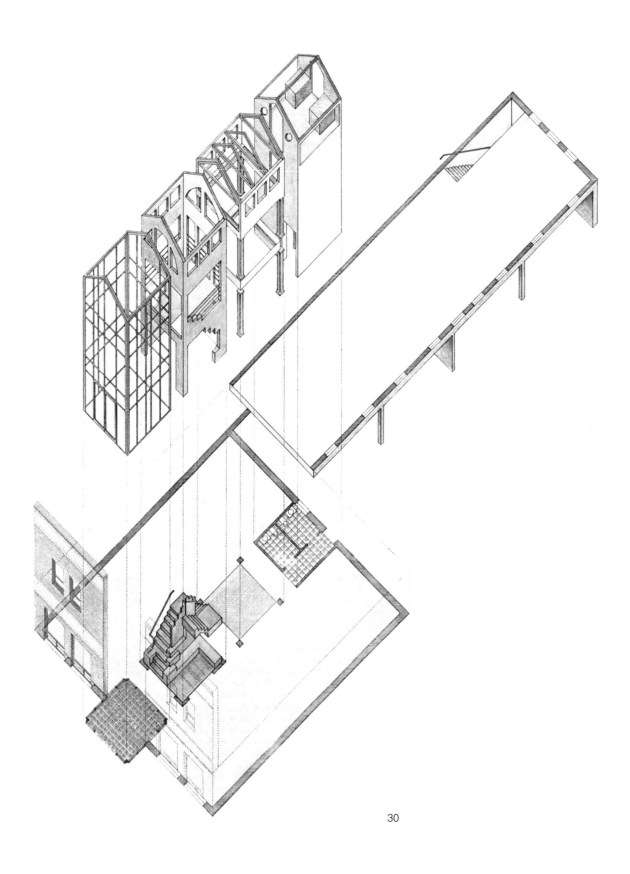

30

Roundhouse Office Building (Renovation), Fort Worth, Texas 1981

31

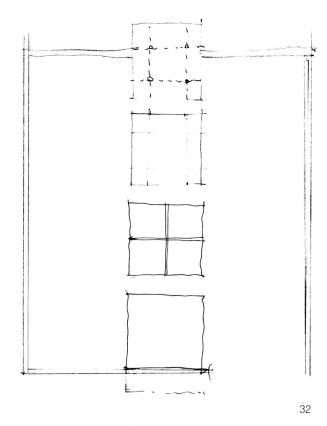

32

Roundhouse Office Building (Renovation), Fort Worth, Texas 1981

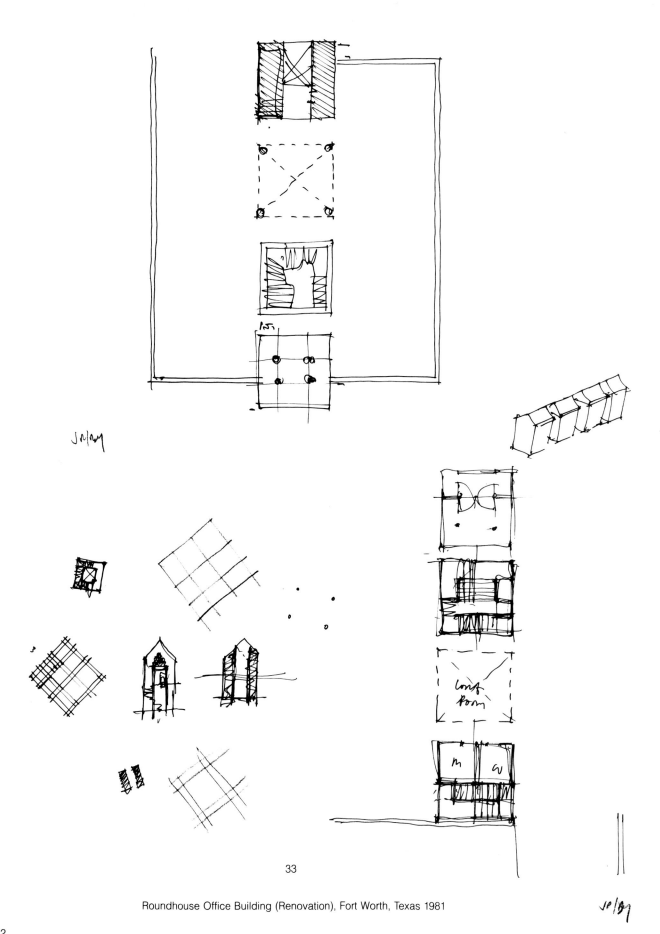

33

Roundhouse Office Building (Renovation), Fort Worth, Texas 1981

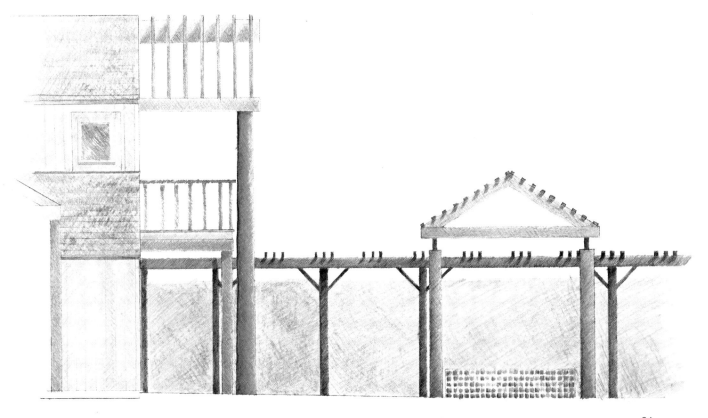

34

Beverly House, Los Angeles, California 1980-1981

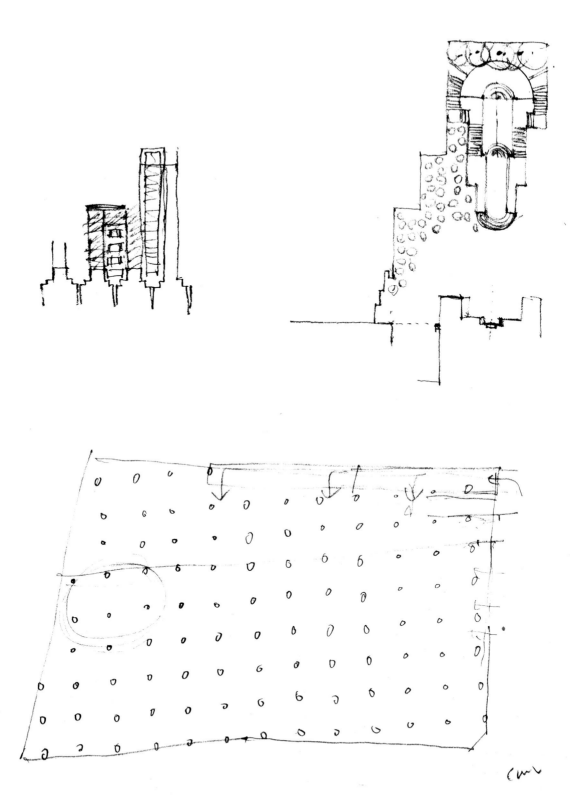

35

Knapp Center Office Building, Los Angeles, California 1981

MOORE RUBLE YUDELL

A partnership established in 1975, Morphosis has developed projects in the United States, Mexico and Africa. The firm has been involved with projects in medicine, civic design, education, multiple- and single-family housing, renovation and exhibition design. Thom Mayne and Michael Rotondi, principals of the firm, hold faculty positions at the Southern California Institute of Architecture. Morphosis has exhibited and been published internationally.

Each project is approached on its own merits. Our aim is to identify and exploit the opportunities inherent in the idiosyncracies within each problem — the aspects that make each one different and unique from any other. The continuity within the body of work has to do with a set of attitudes regarding buildings and language, the relationship of buildings and their settings, and technology or the process by which buildings are made.

LAWRENCE HOUSE

The Lawrence House explores broken expectations. The basis is made up from an element in memory of the original bungalow once on this beach site and an element representative of the modern box building. The former direction of the exterior is developed from a set of rules which dictate a simple system using elements of each type.

The interior has a different and contrary set of rules based on a sequential arrangement of diverse space types. The basis of the project is the dialogue and interaction set up between these two ideas.

HERMOSA BEACH CITY CENTER

The plan intensifies the existing urban core while clarifying and ordering the existing disparate elements. The establishment of new relationships and the reinforcement of existing conditions were joined to develop a continuity of formal spatial arrangements. Particular urban aspects were reinforced:

1. the importance of the pier as a symbolic city element and its organizing power relative to the two sites,
2. the city's desire for a continuity of small scale development and the maintenance of the low heights of buildings which preserve the views for buildings of the hill inland of both sites,
3. the existing grid block urban structure inherent within both sides.

The building complexes on each site perform very different tasks while simultaneously reinforcing the symmetry implicit in the presence of the pier and the streets axial and perpendicular to the pier.

36

Lawrence House, Hermosa Beach, California 1980-1982

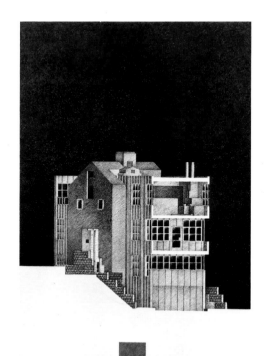

Lawrence House, Hermosa Beach, California 1980-1982

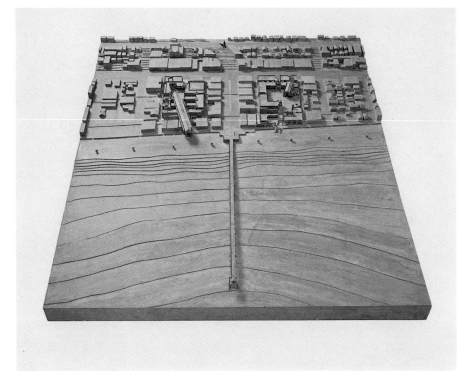

38

Hermosa Center, Hermosa Beach, California 1982

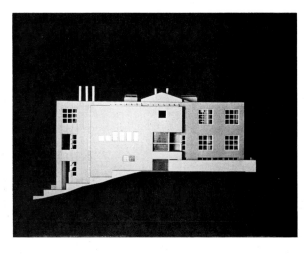

39

40

Lawrence House, Hermosa Beach, California 1980-1982

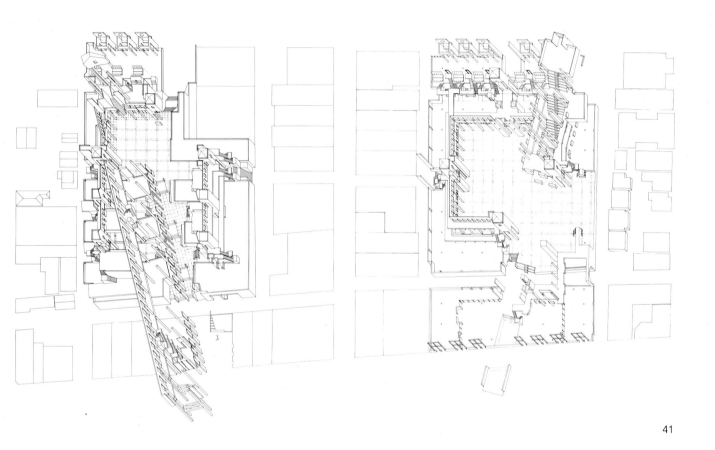

41

Hermosa Center, Hermosa Beach, California 1982

ERIC OWEN MOSS

Born in 1943, Moss received a M.Arch. from both the University of California, Berkeley, in 1968 and from the Graduate School of Design at Harvard in 1972. He has traveled extensively through Europe, the Far East, and South America. A Professor of Design and Member of the Board of Directors at the Southern California Institute of Architecture (SCIARC) since 1974, Moss began private practice in 1976.

THE END OF THE BEGINNING

We live in a time when the self-assured ideological positions of the early twentieth century seem to have blurred. Early practitioners of modern architecture anticipated the coming of a new world for a new man, severed from a dusty, eclectic past, built with clean, functional, "off-the-shelf" parts. This architectural language was fresh and meaningful, particularly as it was understood as an integral component of a social and artistic experience.

Sixty years later this experience has quite obviously been vitiated — still seen, but it is no longer felt. When modern architecture jumped the Atlantic it dropped a large amount of its social content in the sea. Particularly in America, the language of modernism has often been an issue of image, lacking social and cultural moorings. Now, how can architecture proceed when the ideological component is no longer vital, when a collective commitment no longer seems genuine, and when, nevertheless, there remains a residue of the old language, concomitant with perhaps a new one, vigorously preferred, equally artificial?

Conviction must now be totally personal. It is unlikely to find collective sympathy or reinforcement in any current artistic or historic perceptions. An attempt must be made to transcend the now vacuous arguments of modernism; the pseudo-egalitarian morality of context and Route '66, and the uncatholic importation of Rome, while making irreligious use of them all.

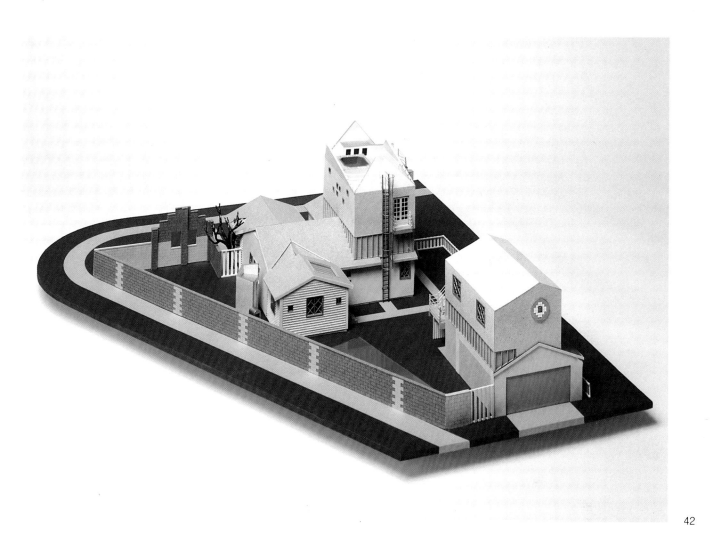

42

43

Culbertson/Petal/Fleur de Lis House, West Los Angeles, California 1981

Fun House, Calabassas (Hidden Valley), Ventura, California 1979   44

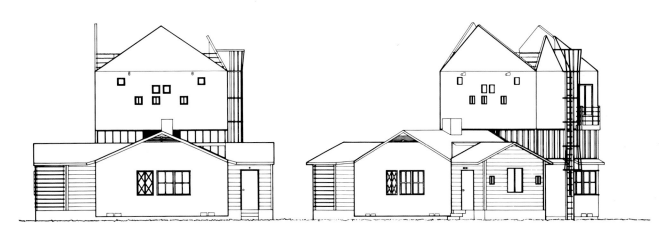

Culbertson/Petal/Fleur de Lis House, West Los Angeles, California 1981   45

Fun House, Calabassas (Hidden Valley), Ventura, California 1979   46

Culbertson/Petal/Fleur de Lis House, West Los Angeles, California 1981   47

Costa Mesa Office, Costa Mesa, California 1981

48

Culbertson/Petal/Fleur de Lis House, West Los Angeles, California 1981

49

ROB WELLINGTON QUIGLEY, AIA

ROB QUIGLEY ARCHITECTS, SAN DIEGO

After receiving his B.Arch. in 1969 from the University of Utah, Quigley served for two years as a Peace Corps Architect in Chile. Active since 1974 with his own firm, he has presented numerous papers on the subject of energy conservation design, and has held faculty positions at the University of California, San Diego. He lectures internationally and his work has appeared in *Abitare, L.A. Architect, Architektur & Wohnen, A+U, Progressive Architecture* and other publications.

Respectful, but mercifully free of the academic clenched teeth to the north, we seek a less pedantic local expression — as concerned with budget and contractors as context and image. Narrative design, schizophrenic collage, and a personal obsession with the hypocrisy of architectural permanence only mildly betray the sun-numbed clichés of our beach life sanctuary.

JAEGER BEACH HOUSE

The site is 150 feet from the beach but surrounded by asphalt drives and isolated from the sea by a continuous wall of dwellings.

Pavilion-like structures rise from this unfortunate reality, optimistically seeking the ocean views and turning inward on themselves away from the encircling rear facades and fences. Locally nostalgic imagery celebrates the wonderful duality of a beach life.

The buildings are organized not by geometry but by the natural forces of the sea ... a symbolic aquatic event leaves in its wake an intimate urban village, magical and faceted in its asphalt setting.

This narrative is a design device used to give the landlocked house an immediacy to the sea and explore the more fundamental issue of permanence in a transient Southern California society.

FIESTA LOW-COST HOUSING

The harsh desert site includes 66 passively designed units clustered around a satellite communication dish.

Flexible "shoe box" spaces allow the buyer and developer interchangeable plans. Traditional suburban notions of public, semi-public and private exterior spaces are respected.

Owners are encouraged to "take possession" of their homes by cultivating the front and rear yards and decorating exterior walls. Rigid site planning, standardized components, and familiar tract-house detailing throughout eliminate on-site thinking.

CHILD LIFE CENTER

Child Life is a small addition to the sprawling Harbor UCLA Medical Complex.

The Child Life Program is a fascinating concept in educational therapy. It strives through play therapy and play activities to address the anxiety and fear a hospital environment evokes in children. The architecture addresses these same concerns. The precise, intimate scale and bouyant use of color are intended to provide an optimistic counterpoint to the alienating and depressing hospital complex behind.

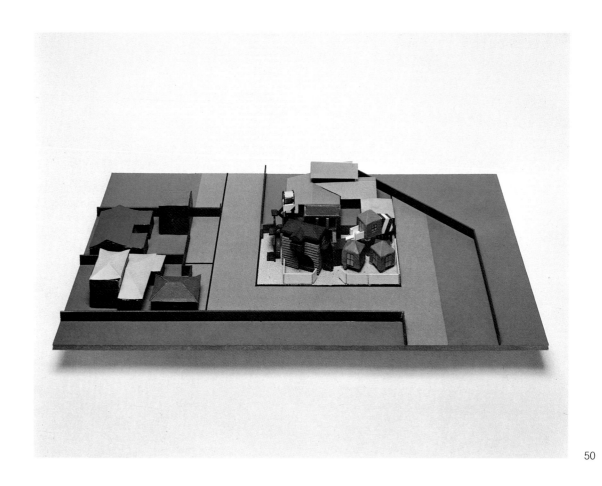

50

51

Jaeger Residence, Del Mar, California 1982

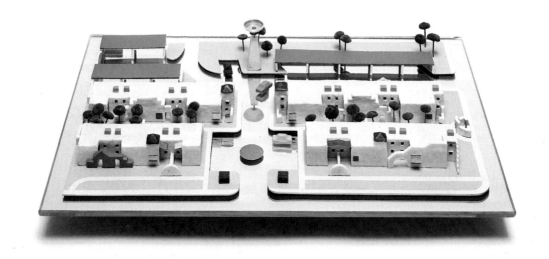

52

Fiesta Park Low Income Housing, Brawley, California 1982

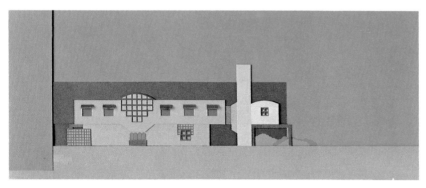

53

Child Life Center, Harbor UCLA Medical Complex, Torrance, California 1982

MICHAEL FRANKLIN ROSS, AIA

Ross received his architectural degrees from Cornell in 1966 and from Columbia University in 1967. Awarded a Fulbright Fellowship in 1972, Ross resided in Japan, served on the Faculty of Tokyo University, and authored a book about Japanese architecture. For fourteen years prior to establishing a private practice, Ross served as Project Architect with several major firms in New York and California. Ross is now a member of the faculty of the Southern California Institute of Architecture and a partner in the firm of Ross/Wou International.

If it is true that architecture is the union of art and science, then our office is a laboratory seeking to create high art through increasingly higher levels of technology. We are explorers with artistic vision. As an architect I perceive myself as an experimenter, employing scientific principles, but guided by an artistic purpose.

My objective is to create places for people that challenge their imaginations and lift their spirits. Noble goals, never easily achieved, but they form the raison d'être for our work. My desire is to titillate and stimulate, to imply the whole through various fragments, then to let the mystery of the architecture unfold in a sequence of discoveries.

I like buildings that becon and attract, but don't give away all their secrets at first glance. I like buildings that are approachable, but that require an investment of time to really understand their inner personality. It's important to see them at different hours of the day and night, in different seasons, and in varying degrees of light.

I am interested in making places that are in harmony with nature, but at the same time employ state-of-the-art technology. I respect trees and sun and natural ventilation, yet I believe it is possible to create an architecture that advances the science of building while esthetically expressing the inner nature of the building itself. Every project by virtue of its site, its surroundings and the purpose it serves develops an inner nature that the architect expresses through the design evolution. This is basic to our work. Every building we design develops an esthetic that is its own in response to its specific situation.

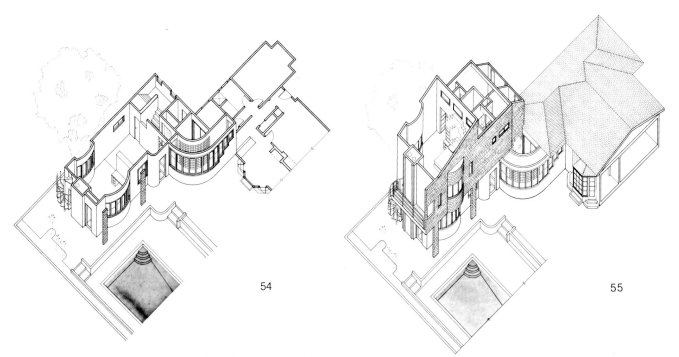

54
55

Greenberg Residence Addition, Sherman Oaks, California 1981-1982

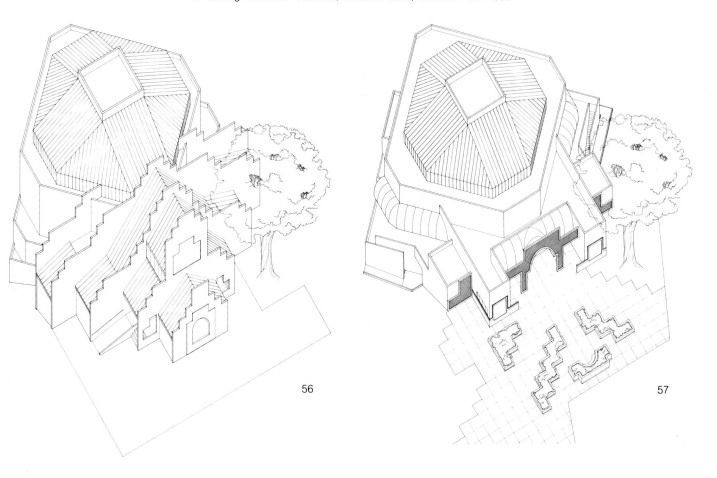

56
57

Solvang Theaterfest, Solvang, California 1982

TED SMITH

Ted Smith received his B.Arch. in 1971 from the University of Virginia. Registered in 1974, he rode the building boom in Southern California designing custom homes and speculative projects. He has lectured at California universities, and his work has been published in California and Europe.

"Blendo" became a big deal to me in the seventies. I dreamed of European streets where buildings flow together but found in San Diego only poor replicas of last month's magazine centerfolds plopped by the architectural flock on 5000-square-foot lots. My project neighbors were various styles from Sea Ranch Modern to California Gwathmy, and my clients flashed dreams from *House Beautiful* and *Architectural Digest*. Attempts at contextual abstraction left me explaining my intentions, so I turned to direct imitation, blending the styles of the houses to the left and right into concoctions I called "contextual."

The Schenck House combines the retaining wall and pole house solutions of adjacent buildings on a steep hillside site. Victor Condo's neighbors are Victorian houses and white industrial boxes. Upas Street is three speculative houses, all identical for economy, that have been rotated to expose different principal facades derived from the neighborhood. All the projects wish they had no edges.

I required my designs to incorporate architectural features I might never have used. The more I studied the surrounding styles, the more I found in each. Before long I couldn't tell good style from bad. My European dreams have faded as all this California clutter has started to look just fine.

The Grove House is a project for a perfect site, no neighbors only trees. I almost didn't know what to make of it.

58

Victor Condo, Carlsbad, California 1979-1980

59

Upas Street/Revolving Houses, San Diego, California 1978-1982

60

Grove House, Vista, California 1981-1982

TED SMITH

THOMAS GORDON SMITH

THOMAS GORDON SMITH AIA, SAN FRANCISCO

Born in 1948 in Oakland, California, Smith received his education at the University of California, Berkeley. A Fellow of the American Academy in Rome (1979), Smith has exhibited internationally. His work has been featured in such publications as *Progressive Architecture*, *Casa Vogue*, *Newsweek* and the *Journal of Architectural Education*.

The most apparent aspect of my architectural work is my commitment to the classical system. I have been working to develop a systematic approach to my use of the classical system based on the inherent hierarchy of the orders. The anthropomorphic associations of the classical elements intrigue me and coincide with my interest in figurative arts and iconography in building programs. What interests me is the challenge of making classicism live again — in a way which is responsive to our time and contributes to the universal tradition of this language.

SPONSORS' PAVILION

When the 1980 Venice Biennale Exhibition of Architetcture "The Presence of the Past" was installed in San Francisco it was primarily funded through the contributions of development corporations and architectural firms. The Sponsors' Pavilion was a place for the contributors to display their building projects and gain recognition for their support of the exhibition.

In order to break down its volume and to provide openings to the adjacent galleries, the pavilion assumed the form of three linked pavilions which represented the Doric, Ionic, and Corinthian orders. Three architectural murals were painted on the facades of each court to make an analogy between First, Second, and Third Style Roman painting and the progression of the classical orders.

RICHMOND HILL HOUSE

Richmond Hill House is built on the brow of a low hill at the edge of San Francisco Bay in Richmond, California. Both in plan and in architectural development the house reflects the notion of hierarchy inherent in the classical system, as well as the development of Roman painting styles. On the exterior, both materials and classical orders are articulated to emphasize the importance of the entrance, progressing from stucco to travertine to marble. The notion of hierarchy is continued upon entry: the foyer is Doric and painted in First Style. The dining-kitchen area is developed as a three-dimensional Second Style painting with an Ionic Order. The living room is an elaborate Corinthian room with walls painted in Third Style fresco. This composition is intended to support the theme of the house: the interdependence of elements of high and low order, and the interdependence of American and European forms.

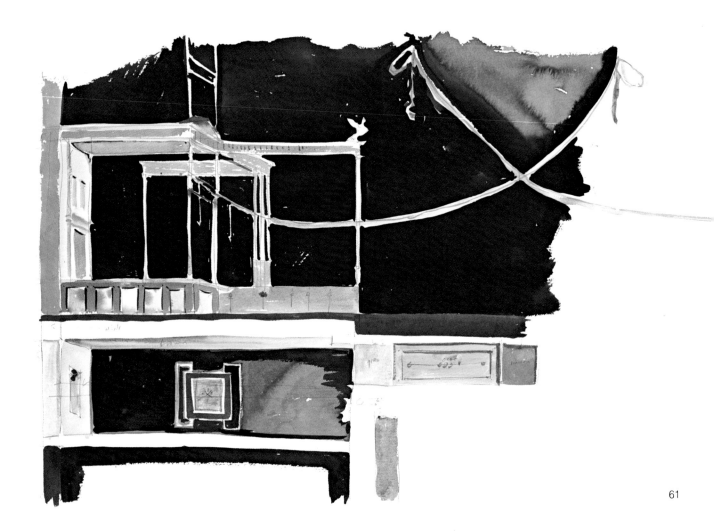

61

Fresco Study from Pompeii, 1980

Charles Garnier - 3rd style study.   6/1/82.

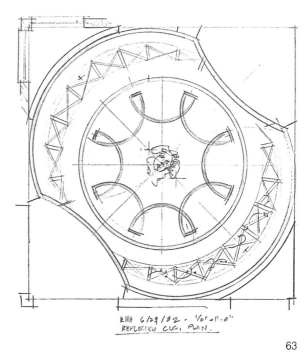

RHH 6/29/82 - 1/8"=1'-0"
REFLECTED CLG. PLAN.

63

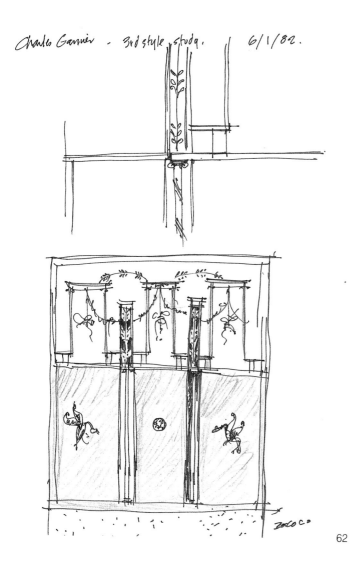

ZOCO Co

62

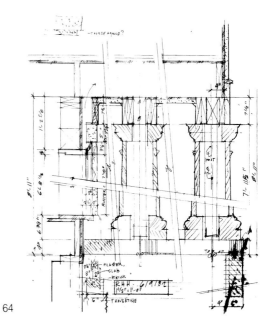

RHH 6/9/82
1 1/2"=1'-0"

64

Richmond Hill House, Richmond, California, 1982

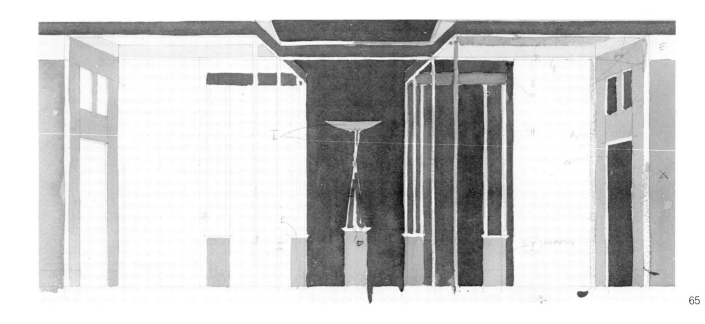

65

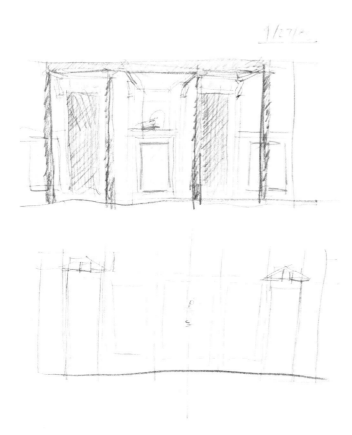

66

Sponsor's Pavilion, The Presence of the Past, San Francisco, California 1982

THOMAS GORDON SMITH

DANIEL SOLOMON AND BARBARA STAUFFACHER-SOLOMON

DANIEL SOLOMON, FAIA/BARBARA STAUFFACHER-SOLOMON, SAN FRANCISCO

Born in 1939 in San Francisco, Daniel Solomon holds degrees from Stanford University (B.A., 1962), Columbia University (B.Arch., 1963), and the University of California, Berkeley (M.Arch., 1966). He is a Professor of Architecture at the University of California, Berkeley and has been in practice with his own firm since 1967.

After a successful career as a graphic designer, Barbara Stauffacher-Solomon received her M. Arch. from the University of California, Berkeley, in 1981. Her thesis on landscape and architecture is now being published (along with an exhibition of drawings) at the Walker Art Center. She has just been awarded a Fellowship for 1983 at the American Academy in Rome.

We are Californians. We live in the out-of-doors and exercise. For us the integration of dwelling and garden and of garden and town is fundamental.

In this collection, the works — house, garden and town — are parts of a picture. During our lifetimes it is the idea of town that has suffered most from the activities of architects during thirty years which stand apart from the previous one thousand. We therefore like to feel part of a collective, worldwide movement to re-establish historical continuity in the growth of towns. Our conceptions of dwelling and garden serve a re-emergent sense of town.

HOUSE

Le Corbusier gave words and shapes to ideas that were latent and irresistible. After sixty years many conditions remain unchanged. Now, as earlier, practically no one can afford to have very much. The art and common sense of the white house remain overpowering, but it was the imperative of these houses that did in our sense of civics. Now the white houses in their intelligence and severtiy are no longer welcome like the soldiers of a liberating army. To live in the town, they must become citizens and observe old ways. DS

TOWN

Our short urban history sits lightly. Petaluma, Balboa, St. Helena, Sonoma, Sebastopol, Calistoga, Laguna Beach, Seal Beach, San Francisco are fragile. There are many threats. In California place and no-place are locked in struggle. We now stand at a peculiar point, for it is in our hands to decide whether or not we shall have a history. Perhaps it is the *genius loci* of California to be perpetually new. Some people think that the best process — one which captures the essence of the place — obliterates obsolescence in a present of eternally gleaming novelty. To us this seems untrue. Our present is redolent with nostalgia, sometimes for the 1940's, sometimes for the 16th century. Our works of architecture and planning are about the self-conscious retention of past in a process of rapid and radical changes. DS

GARDEN

Since practically no one can afford to have very much dwelling these days, public and semi-private recreational gardens can provide some of that paradise lost. The amenities that won't fit into the individual budget or lot can be realized in the collective park/paradise. Even God, content to be in the details for many years, now yearns to return to the garden. We in California are obsessed with nature and with paradise. For us nature as paradise is the recreational garden. We use it to improve our bodies, incidentally our minds and certainly our chances for immortality. In the cities we can decide that a selected rectangle in the grid will be gre⁀ We make a park. We make a palm. It is a green theatre for playi playacting. BSS

67

e Garden—Urban Garden: No. 1 1982

68

The Garden—Tied Palm Tree: No. 3: The Palm is Paradise Series 1982

The Town—Crissy Field Project, San Francisco, California 1979

69

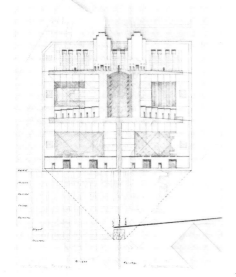

70

The Town—South Beach Housing No. 1,
San Francisco, California 1982

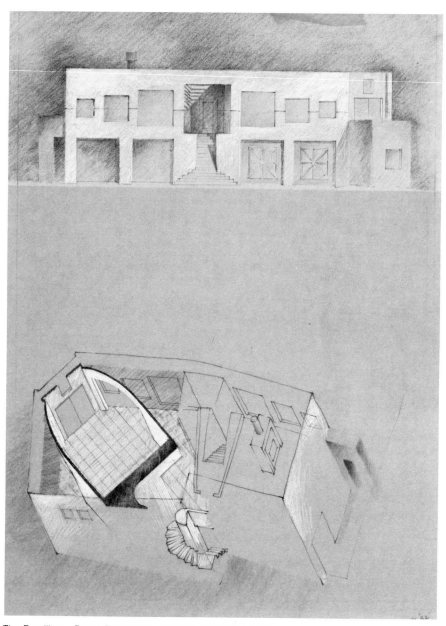

71

The Dwelling—Byrne Residence, Del Mar, California 1982

72

The Dwelling—Union Court, San Francisco, California 1982

WILLIAM TURNBULL, JR.

MLTW/TURNBULL ASSOCIATES, SAN FRANCISCO

Born in 1935 in New York City, Turnbull received architectural degrees from Princeton University (B.A., 1956; M.F.A., 1959) and the Diplôme of the Ecole des Beaux Arts de Fontainebleau (1956). He is a Fellow of the American Institute of Architects and the American Academy in Rome. Director of MLTW/Turnbull Associates since 1970, Turnbull is currently an Architectural Critic at the University of California, Berkeley.

We believe architecture is primarily concerned with establishing a "sense of place," whether its inspiration is derived from the idiosyncracies of a particular landscape or the pragmatic requirements of an individual client.

Each building requires a perceptive insight and ordering idea. At Woodrun Place we were concerned with the appropriateness of a man-made object on a difficult site in a spectacular mountain landscape. We seized upon an image of a European masonry farmhouse. From that starting point, the building became the resolution of new layers and changes in the client's program and the town's demands.

Other buildings are born from compelling metaphors such as the Malibu Residence: "A House within a Garden within a House." We are intrigued with the idea of buildings as geodes, full of twists and inversions.

The Healdsburg Residence and Fisher Winery come closer to describing the general work of our office. The Winery is concerned with the love of making things, in this case the craft of heavy timber construction. This is coupled with the delight of economy of means (the barrel racks are structural columns). The Healdsburg Residence is more arcane. Here the response to a landscape recalls classical sites of the Aegean area, and hence the simple temple form. The form, however is not a copy, but a symbol of shelter similar to the barn forms which mark the agricultural landscape. Under the roof the plan responds to the variety of program, relationship and view. The sunrise/sunset pediments remind us that architecture can also incorporate humor and wit, as well as more pragmatic elements.

Place-making, then, is concerned with the appropriateness of a building in a landscape and with the enjoyment of the people that inhabit our buildings. Architecture is space and light to intrigue the mind and delight the eye.

73

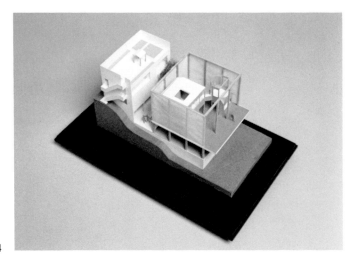

74

75

Naegele Residence, Malibu, California 1981

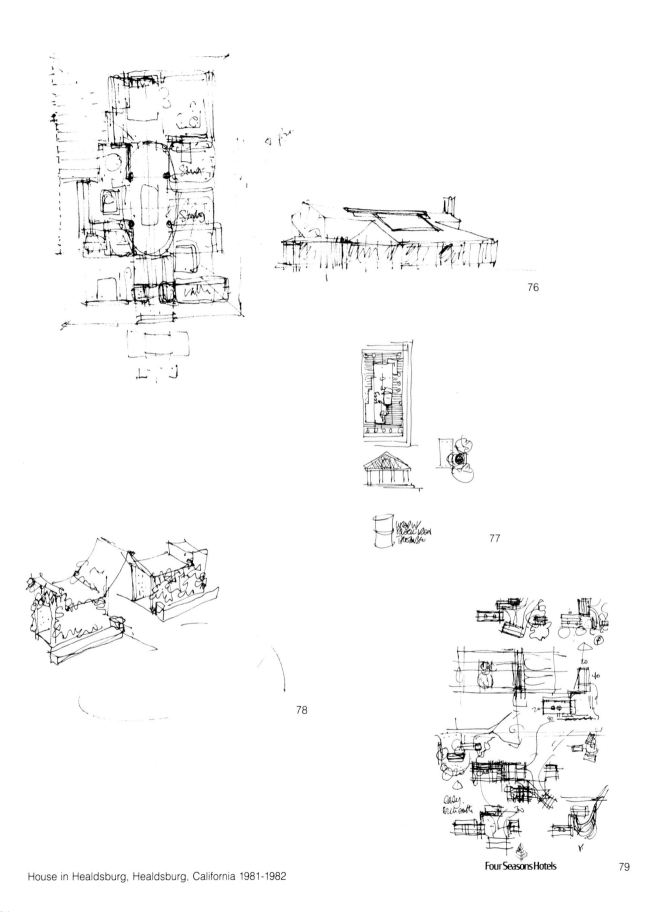

76

77

78

Four Seasons Hotels 79

House in Healdsburg, Healdsburg, California 1981-1982

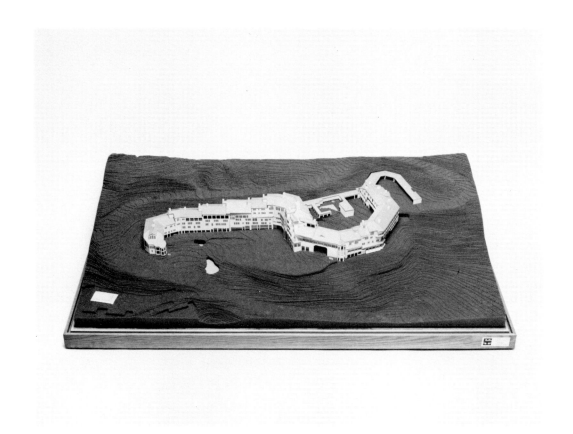

80

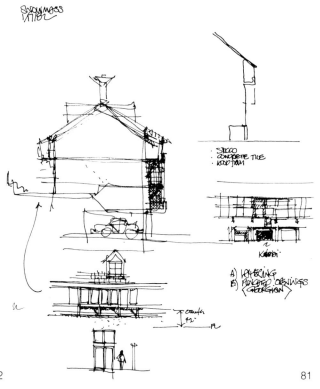

Woodrun Place, Snowmass Village, Colorado 1982

81

CATALOGUE LIST

Dimensions are given in inches; height precedes width; width precedes depth.

FRANK O. GEHRY

BEVERLY HILLS RESIDENCE, Beverly Hills, California

1 Early Model 1981
  mixed media
  12″ x 41″ x 16½″
  Credits: Frank O. Gehry and Associates

2 Sketch 1980
  ink on paper
  10¾″ x 8″
  Private Collection, Los Angeles
  Credits: Frank O. Gehry and Associates

3 Sketch 1981
  ink on paper
  10¾″ x 8″
  Private Collection, Los Angeles
  Credits: Frank O. Gehry and Alejo

4 Later Model (front elevation) 1981-1982
  mixed media
  12″ x 41″ x 12½″
  Credits: Frank O. Gehry and Associates

5 Sketch 1982
  ink on paper
  8″ x 10¾″
  Private Collection, Los Angeles
  Credits: Frank O. Gehry and Associates

6 Sketch 1981
  ink on paper
  10¾″ x 8″
  Private Collection, Los Angeles
  Credits: Frank O. Gehry and Associates

7 Later Model (side elevation) 1981-1982
  mixed media
  12″ x 41″ x 17½″
  Credits: Frank O. Gehry and Associates

THE LOYOLA LAW SCHOOL, Los Angeles, California

8 Model 1981
  mixed media
  8″ x 43″ x 28″
  Credits: Frank O. Gehry and Associates

9 Model 1981
  mixed media
  8″ x 43″ x 28″
  Credits: Frank O. Gehry and Associates

CALIFORNIA AEROSPACE MUSEUM, Venice, California

10 Sketch 1982
   ink on paper
   8″ x 10¾″
   Credits: Frank O. Gehry and Associates

11 Model 1982
   mixed media
   4″ x 25″ x 29″
   Credits: Frank O. Gehry and Associates

12 Sketch 1982
   ink on paper
   10¾″ x 8″
   Credits: Frank O. Gehry and Associates

13 Sketch 1982
   ink on paper
   8″ x 10¾″
   Credits: Frank O. Gehry and Associates

TOM GRONDONA

SASKA'S "STAR OF THE SIDEWALK," San Diego, California

14 Model 1981-1982
   mixed media
   16″ x 13″ x 10″
   Credits: Architecture by Tom Grondona; Structural Engineer,
   Bob Fefferman; Restaurant Consultant, Dave Saska

KISSING CASTLES

15 Model 1982
   mixed media
   96″ x 120″ x 156″
   Credits: Architecture by Tom Grondona; Model Makers, Ben Grondona,
   Mary Grondona, Ruthie Brownlee, Robbie Nelson, Bruce Peeling
   and Dave Saska

PROJECT (CHÂTEAU EXPLOSIF), Point Loma, California

16 Model 1982
   mixed media
   60″ x 24″ x 24″

FRANK ISRAEL

BAMBOO BUNGALOWS, Manila, Philippines

17 Elevation Drawings 1980
ink on paper
36" x 20"
Credits: Frank Israel

18 Roof Plan and Elevation Drawing 1980
ink on paper
36" x 20"
Credits: Frank Israel

19 Model 1980
bamboo
13¼" x 11½" x 12½"
Credits: Frank Israel

20 Site Plan 1980
ink on paper
36" x 20"
Credits: Frank Israel

STUDIO FOR AN ARTIST, New York, New York

21 Floor Plan 1980-1982
ink on paper
36" x 20"
Credits: Frank Israel

BELLISLE RANCH, Santa Barbara, California

22 Model 1980
mixed media
3" x 12¼" x 31½"
Credits: Frank Israel

ANTHONY J. LUMSDEN

CHANGI HOTEL, Singapore, Singapore

23 Model 1980
stained wood
5½" x 21⅝" x 21½"
Credits: Architect, Anthony J. Lumsden; Project Manager,
Paul Chikamori; Design Assistant, Ignacio Gonzalez

ENCINO OFFICE BUILDING, Encino, California

24 Model 1981
wood
6" x 36" x 18"
Credits: Architect, Anthony J. Lumsden; Project Manager, Stephan Mann;
Assistant Designers, Petrus Smulders, Simon Locke and Dick Matteson

SACRAMENTO OFFICE BUILDING, Sacramento, California

25 Model 1982
mixed media
24" x 24" x 24"
Credits: Architect, Anthony J. Lumsden; Assistant Designer, Kim Day

26 Model 1982
mixed media
24" x 24" x 24"
Credits: Architect, Anthony J. Lumsden; Assistant Designer, Kim Day

KNAPP CENTER, Los Angeles, California

27 Model 1981
crescent board
18" x 36" x 24½"
Credits: Architect, Anthony J. Lumsden; Assistant Designer, Kim Day

RAHARDJA CENTER, Singapore, Singapore

28 Model 1981
white plexiglass
16" x 21¼" x 21¼"
Credits: Architect, Anthony J. Lumsden; Project Manager, Paul Chikamori;
Assistant Designers, Kim Day, Ignacio Gonzalez, Fred Lappin
and Petrus Smulders

29 Model (detail) 1981
white plexiglass
16" x 21¼" x 21¼"
Credits: Architect, Anthony J. Lumsden; Project Manager, Paul Chikamori;
Assistant Designers, Kim Day, Ignacio Gonzalez, Fred Lappin
and Petrus Smulders

CHARLES MOORE, JOHN RUBLE AND BUZZ YUDELL

ROUNDHOUSE OFFICE BUILDING (Renovation),
Fort Worth, Texas

30 Axonometric Drawing 1981
colored pencil on vellum
24" x 23¾"
Credits: Moore Ruble Yudell: John Ruble, Buzz Yudell and Tina Beebe

31 Axonometric Drawing 1981
colored pencil on paper
36" x 24"
Credits: Moore Ruble Yudell: John Ruble, Buzz Yudell and Tina Beebe

32 Sketch 1981
pen on tracing paper
12″ x 12″
Credits: Moore Ruble Yudell: Charles Moore, Buzz Yudell
and Tina Beebe

33 Sketches (three) 1981
pen on tracing paper
12″ x 12″ each
Credits: Moore Ruble Yudell: John Ruble, Buzz Yudell
and Tina Beebe

BEVERLY HOUSE, Los Angeles, California

34 Elevation Drawing 1980-1981
colored pencil on paper
16″ x 21″
Credits: Moore Ruble Yudell: Design Architect, Buzz
Yudell with
Charles Jencks and Tina Beebe

KNAPP CENTER OFFICE BUILDING, Los Angeles,
California

35 Sketches (three) 1981
pencil and ink on paper
12″ x 14″ each
Credits: Moore Ruble Yudell, Charles Moore, Buzz
Yudell and Tina Beebe

MORPHOSIS (THOM MAYNE AND MICHAEL ROTONDI)

LAWRENCE HOUSE, Hermosa Beach, California

36 Elevation Drawings (four in a series of nine) 1980-1982
pencil on paper
30″ x 22″ each
Credits: Thom Mayne and Michael Rotondi with
Benjamin Caffey,
Frank Lupo and Kazu Arai

37 Elevation Drawings (four in a series of nine) 1980-1982
pencil on paper
30″ x 22″ each
Credits: Thom Mayne and Michael Rotondi with
Benjamin Caffey,
Frank Lupo and Kazu Arai

HERMOSA CENTER, Hermosa Beach, California

38 Model 1982
cardboard and modeling paste
15″ x 52″ x 44″
Credits: Thom Mayne and Michael Rotondi with Gian
Luigi Irsonti
and Kazu Arai

LAWRENCE HOUSE, Hermosa Beach, California

39 Model, Front Elevation 1980-1982
foamcore board
15″ x 16½″ x 27⅞″
Credits: Thom Mayne and Michael Rotondi with
Benjamin Caffey,
Frank Lupo and Kazu Arai

40 Model, Side Elevation 1980-1982
foamcore board
15″ x 16½″ x 27⅞″
Credits: Thom Mayne and Michael Rotondi with
Benjamin Caffey,
Frank Lupo and Kazu Arai

HERMOSA CENTER, Hermosa Beach, California

41 Axonometric Drawing 1982
ink on linen
36″ x 42″
Credits: Thom Mayne and Michael Rotondi with Gian
Luigi Irsonti
and Kazu Arai

ERIC OWEN MOSS

CULBERTSON/PETAL/FLEUR DE LIS HOUSE, West Los
Angeles, California

42 Model 1981
mixed media
8″ x 30¾″ x 28″
Credits: Eric Owen Moss, Nick Seirup and Frank
Daniel

43 Elevation Drawings (two in a series of eight) 1981
pen and ink
9½″ x 121″
Credits: Eric Owen Moss, Nick Seirup and Frank
Daniel

FUN HOUSE, Calabassas (Hidden Valley), Ventura,
California

44 Model (front) 1979
mixed media
11″ x 40″ x 20″
Credits: Eric Owen Moss, Nick Seirup, Roy Barris,
Maritza Culbertson and Frank Daniel

CULBERTSON/PETAL/FLEUR DE LIS HOUSE, West Los
Angeles, California

45 Elevation Drawings (two in a series of eight) 1981
pen and ink
9½″ x 121″
Credits: Eric Owen Moss, Nick Seirup and Frank
Daniel

FUN HOUSE, Calabassas (Hidden Valley), Ventura, California

46 Model (back) 1979
mixed media
11″ x 40″ x 20″
Credits: Eric Owen Moss, Nick Seirup, Roy Barris, Maritza Culbertson and Frank Daniel

CULBERTSON/PETAL/FLEUR DE LIS HOUSE, West Los Angeles, California

47 Elevation Drawings (two in a series of eight) 1981
pen and ink
9½″ x 121″
Credits: Eric Owen Moss, Nick Seirup and Frank Daniel

COSTA MESA OFFICE, Costa Mesa, California

48 Courtyard 1981
pen and ink
24″ x 36″
Credits: Eric Owen Moss, Nick Seirup and Frank Daniel

CULBERTSON/PETAL/FLEUR DE LIS HOUSE, West Los Angeles, California

49 Elevation Drawings (two in a series of eight) 1981
pen and ink
9½″ x 121″
Credits: Eric Owen Moss, Nick Seirup and Frank Daniel

ROB WELLINGTON QUIGLEY
JAEGER RESIDENCE, Del Mar, California

50 Study Model 1982
mixed media
2¼″ x 18½″ x 11″
Credits: Architect, Rob Quigley; Model Makers, Bill Behun,
Bob Dickens and Maryanne Chase

51 Study Model 1982
cardboard
8″ x 35″ x 20½″
Credits: Architect, Rob Quigley; Model Makers, Bill Behun,
Bob Dickens and Maryanne Chase

FIESTA PARK LOW INCOME HOUSING, Brawley, California

52 Study Model 1982
clay
2″ x 16¾″ x 11¼″
Credits: Architect, Rob Quigley; Model Makers, Mario Lara,
Mel McGee and Bob Dickens; Illustrator, Mel McGee; Assistant, Maryanne Chase

CHILD LIFE CENTER, Harbor UCLA Medical Complex, Torrance, California

53 Front Elevation 1982
pantone paper
11″ x 27″
Credits: Architect, Rob Quigley; Illustrator, Mel McGee; Assistant, Maryanne Chase

MICHAEL FRANKLIN ROSS
GREENBERG RESIDENCE ADDITION, Sherman Oaks, California

54 Axonometric First Floor 1981
ink on vellum
25½″ x 30″
Credits: Architect, Michael Franklin Ross; Axonometric First Floor Drawing by Matthew Pickner

55 Axonometric Second Floor 1982
ink on vellum
25″ x 30″
Credits: Architect, Michael Franklin Ross; Axonometric Second Floor Drawing by Hilario Ng

SOLVANG THEATERFEST, Solvang, California

56 Preliminary Design Axonometric 1982
ink on vellum
30″ x 25″
Credits: A joint venture of Ross Associates and Flood, Meyer,
Sutton & Associates: Principles in charge, Michael Franklin Ross
and Douglas B. Meyer; Drawings by Deeing Chu

57 Final Design Axonometric 1982
ink on vellum
30″ x 25″
Credits: A joint venture of Ross Associates and Flood, Meyer, Sutton & Associates: Principles in charge, Michael Franklin Ross and Douglas B. Meyer; Drawing by Deeing Chu

TED SMITH

VICTOR CONDO, Carlsbad, California
California

58 Model 1979-1980
mixed media
22½" x 25½" x 5½"
Credits: Ted Smith and Kathleen McCormick

UPAS STREET/REVOLVING HOUSES, San Diego,
California

59 Model 1978-1982
mixed media
30" x 30" x 24"
Credits: Ted Smith, Kathleen McCormick and John
Oleinick

GROVE HOUSE, Vista, California

60 Model 1981-1982
mixed media
13" x 48" x 35"
Credits: Ted Smith and Kathleen McCormick

THOMAS GORDON SMITH

FRESCO STUDY FROM POMPEII,
House of the Orchard, Pompeii

61 House of the Orchard, Third Style Room 1980
watercolor on paper
19" x 26"
Credits: Thomas Gordon Smith

RICHMOND HILL HOUSE, Richmond, California

62 Preliminary Sketch 1982
ink and colored pencil on paper
9" x 7½" each
Credits: Architect, Thomas Gordon Smith; Structural
Engineers,
Peter Cully and Associates

63 Preliminary Sketch 1982
ink and colored pencil on paper
9" x 7½"
Credits: Architect, Thomas Gordon Smith; Structural
Engineers,
Peter Cully and Associates

64 Design Development Drawing 1982
pencil on tracing paper
9" x 7¾"
Credits: Architect, Thomas Gordon Smith; Structural
Engineers,
Peter Cully and Associates

SPONSOR'S PAVILION, THE PRESENCE OF THE PAST,
San Francisco, California

65 Preliminary Sketch/Working Drawing 1982
Watercolor on paper
8" x 20"
Credits: Thomas Gordon Smith

66 Preliminary Sketch/Working Drawing 1982
ink and colored pencil
9" x 7¾"
Credits: Thomas Gordon Smith

DANIEL SOLOMON/BARBARA STAUFFACHER-SOLOMON

THE GARDEN

67 *URBAN GARDEN:* No. 1 1982
colored pencil on vellum
10" x 8"
Credits: Barbara Stauffacher-Solomon

68 *TIED PALM TREE:* No. 3: THE PALM IS PARADISE
SERIES 1982
colored pencil on vellum
12" x 8½"
Credits: Barbara Stauffacher-Solomon

THE DWELLING

69 *CRISSY FIELD PROJECT,* San Francisco, California

Map 1979
colored pencil on vellum
11" x 8½"
Credits: Barbara Stauffacher-Solomon

70 *SOUTH BEACH HOUSING No. 1,* San Francisco,
California

Site Plan with Elevations 1982
colored pencil on vellum
11" x 8½"
Credits: Daniel Solomon, Barbara
Stauffacher-Solomon, Paulett Taggart

THE TOWN

71 *BYRNE RESIDENCE,* Del Mar, California

Elevation and Axonometric Drawings 1982
colored pencil on tracing paper
12" x 9"
Credits: Architect, Daniel Solomon; Project Associate,
John Long

72 *UNION COURT,* San Francisco, California
　　Model 1981
　　paper
　　11″ x 14⅝″ x 21¼″
　　Credits: Architect, Daniel Solomon and Paulett Taggart

WILLIAM TURNBULL, JR.

NAEGELE RESIDENCE, Malibu, California

73 Study Model 1981
　　strathmore board, colored paper and cardboard
　　6⅛″ x 12½″ x 6⅛″
　　Credits: William Turnbull, Jr., with Henry Siegel and
　　Richard Sol

74 Study Model 1981
　　strathmore board, colored paper and cardboard
　　6⅛″ x 12½″ x 6⅛″
　　Credits: William Turnbull, Jr., with Henry Siegel and
　　Richard Sol

75 Sketch of Interior Ruin 1981
　　felt tip on white paper
　　4″ x 7″
　　Credits: William Turnbull, Jr., with Henry Siegel and
　　Richard Sol

HOUSE IN HEALDSBURG, Healdsburg, California

76 Preliminary Study Sketch 1981
　　felt tip on tracing paper
　　6″ x 8″
　　Credits: William Turnbull, Jr., with Michael Hull

77 Preliminary Study Sketch 1981
　　felt tip on white paper
　　5″ x 3″
　　Credits: William Turnbull, Jr., with Michael Hull

78 Gatehouse Study 1982
　　felt tip on white paper
　　5″ x 6¾″
　　Credits: William Turnbull, Jr., with Michael Hull

79 Conceptual Study, (Caretaker House) 1981
　　felt tip on stationery
　　5⅞″ x 3⅞″
　　Credits: William Turnbull, Jr., with Michael Hull and
　　Heather Trossman

WOODRUN PLACE, Snowmass Village, Colorado

80 Model 1982
　　strathmore board and colored paper
　　9″ x 54″ x 31″
　　Credits: Architect, William Turnbull, Jr.; Project
　　Architect,
　　Hildegard A. Richardson; Project Team, Richard
　　Hocking,
　　Geoff Butler, Mar La Roche, Greg Chiselko and Jane
　　Hendricks

81 Elevation Study Sketch 1982
　　felt tip on white paper
　　10½″ x 8″
　　Credits: Architect, William Turnbull, Jr.; Project
　　Architect,
　　Hildegard A. Richardson; Project Team, Richard
　　Hocking,
　　Geoff Butler, Mar La Roche, Greg Chiselko and Jane
　　Hendricks

STAFF
Sebastian J. Adler/Director
Chris Bartholomew/Curatorial Assistant
Robin Bright/Preparator
Alan Brown/Gardener
Beulah Carmack/Assistant Bookkeeper
Janet Ciaffone/Administrative Assistant
John Ciaffone/Weekend Security
Bolton Colburn/Registrar
Tom Flowers/Building Maintenance
Lynda Forsha/Curator
Rush George Glick/Security
Michael Golino/Building Manager
Russell Hilbert/Woodshop Manager
Prudence Hutshing/Public Information Officer
Greg Kahn/Curator of Film
Constantine Kapsokavadis/Chief Security
Karla Kobrich/Executive Secretary
Racthel Lindgren/Finance Officer
Verna Loy/Museum Bookstore Manager
Frank Maloney/Main Security
Kelly Maloney/Security
Connie O'Neal/Curatorial Assistant
Betty Patterson/Information Desk Receptionist
Gail Richardson/Librarian
Jill Riveroll/Receptionist
Robert Schueler/Auditorium Manager
Bob Scott/Weekend Security
Shannon Spiess/Membership Coordinator
Jesse Tarin/Maintenance
Carol Vidstrand/Weekend Receptionist
Carl Widney/Museum Bookstore Assistant

CREDITS

Design:	Mary Farris, San Diego
Typography:	Line by Line, San Diego
Lithography:	Frye & Smith, San Diego
Photography:	John Durant, San Diego
Edition of:	3,000

Photographers are cited alphabetically,
and credits are cited by page number.

Bielenberg: 23, Fig. 10.
Ruthie Brownlee: 46.
Glenn M. Christiansen: 92.
Tom Grondona: 48.
Reverdy Johnson: 17, Fig. 3
Kathleen McCormick: 80.
Tod Marder; 83.
Douglas M. Parker: 41, 42, 43, 44, 45.
Roy Porello: 26, Fig. 20.
Rob Quigley: 24, Fig. 14.
Marvin Rand: 68, 69.
Gerry Ratto; 20, Fig. 7 and 91.
Ted Smith: 27, Fig. 26 and 27.
Tim Street-Porter: 17, Fig. 2.
Rob Super: 26, Fig. 22 and 23.
Wayne Thom Associates: 23, Fig. 12.
Steven Tomko: 44.